# Yesteryear at the Uniontown Speedway

*Marci Lynn McGuinness*

The *Yesteryear* series by Marci Lynn McGuinness:

*Yesteryear in Ohiopyle,* Volume I

*Yesteryear In Ohiopyle,* Volume II

*Yesteryear in Ohiopyle,* Volume III

*Yesteryear in Masontown,* Volume I

*Yesteryear in Smithfield/Point Marion*

*Yesteryear at the Uniontown Speedway*

*Yesteryear in Ohiopyle* - The Movie

Shore Publications
P. O. Box 26
Chalk Hill, Pennsylvania 15421

 ISBN #978-0-938833-27-7

Second Printing 1996
Third Printing 2008

# Publisher's Message

Dear Readers:

Just five years after Carl Fisher built the Indianapolis 500 Race Track in 1911, the Uniontown, Pennsylvania area Coal and Steel Barons built the Uniontown Speedway. That was 1916, and never has there been more excitement or money flowing through Fayette's County Seat as there was during the peak of the famous board track.

Picture this - Men work feverishly to build a wooden race track just off the National Road (Route 40) in Hopwood and in two months time, race car drivers and film stars of international fame descend to the foot of Summit Mountain for the opening race. Universal Film Studios of New York sponsored races between the best drivers our country had to offer, such as Barney Oldfield, Ralph DePalma, and Gaston, Louis, and Arthur Chevrolet. Special trains brought thousands of fans to the Hopwood track located in the meadow that lies behind the old Commonwealth Marketing, Inc. building At this time, Uniontown boasted over two dozen millionaires as the coal & coke boom was in full swing with Europe at war. Local hotels, restaurants, and theatres overflowed with customers as up to 50,000 people gathered to watch the dare devil drivers. Those days only the elite had automobiles which made the races enormous events as the curious flocked to the Uniontown Speedway boardtrack.

After the Thanksgiving Day Opening Race was delayed because of rain, the track made it's debut on December 2, a bright sunny Monday, when one of racing history's worst tragedies occurred.

This book covers all of the races held at the famous track in addition to chapters on the Summit Mountain Hill Climbs and two later Uniontown Speedways. I do hope you enjoy racing back in time!

To: William Blaney,

Sincerely,

Marci Lynn McGuinness, Publisher
Shore Publications

2011

Note - The automobile names such as Ford, Packard, etc. do not have the ® symbol because there are just too many. I am acknowledging the trademarks in this note.

# Dedication

I would like to dedicate this book to the late Jim Boyd of Jockey Hollow, who befriended me in his late years. Jim and I enjoyed exchanging local history finds and one day a few years ago, we were sitting at his kitchen table going over some Somerfield post cards. Jim had grown up under the town which is now under the Yough Dam on Route 40 East, and lived out his life in a house above Jockey Hollow. This day he had a particularly sly grin that went ear to ear and his eyes were twinkling. He was even giggling a little when he asked me if I had ever heard of the wooden race track that used to be in Hopwood. I had not.

He was clutching a folder to his chest and my curiosity was taking over when I said, "Quit teasing and let's see what you have there.!

He gave me a little background with at least a half dozen photographs of the Uniontown Speedway Boardtrack. Over the next few years he found various shots and let me make copies of them because he was the kind of guy who like seeing things in print and had faith that I would do him justice if he shared with me.

This book is for you, Jim. Thanks for everything...especially the memories.

I would also like to dedicate this book to James "Bender" Bendishaw, who was so excited when I showed him the book, he giggled like Jim Boyd.:) We are racing on, but it isn't as much fun without you!

# Contributors

I would like to thank the following who contributed unselfishly to this publication:

Jim Boyd, Anne Hickey, Louise Clemmer, William Roby, Mack Hinkle, Mel Minnick, Gus & Mary Kay Stickel, Debbie & Mike Konechny, Gary Sisson, Terry Chris, Dr. Regis Maher, Adelaide Wolfe, Dan Bryson, Lois Mitchell and Mike Shafer.

# Contents

# Yesteryear at the Summit Mountain Hill Climbs

This unknown driver is leaning into the first turn of the infamous Turkey's Nest "S" Curve during 1915's all-professional Summit Mountain Hill Climb. Four thousand fans gathered up the mountainside to watch drivers force the "open-air" vehicles to the top. The temporary fences shown were put up to keep spectators off of the National Pike. Notice the men on the telephone pole and the row of them in front of the fence on the right. This was the last Summit Mountain Hill Climb.

# The First Summit Mountain Hill Climb – 1913

In 1902, George Titlow brought the first automobiles to Uniontown, Pennsylvania. By 1911, there were a mere 600,000 automobiles operating in the United States. These were open-air touring models run on steam, gasoline and electricity. A week-long Old Home Week celebration was held in Uniontown in 1912 where many automobiles and even small air craft were on hand to wow local residents. It was this celebratory atmosphere that prompted the Fayette County Automobile Club to organize the first Summit Mountain Hill Climb. The mountain was as it is today, an excellent test for an engine's endurance and power, and this race was the beginning of the racing bug that led to the building of the Uniontown Speedway Boardtrack.

In 1913, Henry Ford introduced the conveyer belt to factory operation and greatly increased the production of motor cars. It was this year that the first annual amateur hill climb was held on June 20 on the east side of Summit Mountain where the course ran 1.1 miles. A crowd of over 4,000 lined the National Road from the bottom of the hill to the top of the Summit where at least 800 cars parked to watch the men. Before the event began, Gus Burke of Pittsburgh was thrown to the ground after riding on the gasoline tank while demonstrating his Hup. Burke was trying the car out with R.H. Richardson, stripped. They had just started up the Summit Mountain from Hopwood when taking a sharp bend threw Burke onto the road with some force. Richardson did not realize he lost his buddy for a few seconds. When he went back to rescue him, Burke was face down and unconscious with blood flowing from a deep wound on his forehead. He was quickly lifted into the vehicle and rushed to town where Dr. Baum took care of his head injury and dislocated shoulder. Burke came to and livened up enough to help his partner give several excellent exhibitions. During the race there were no accidents to mar the day.

A platform was built at the end of the course on top of the mountain where the officials were seated. The judges were William McClelland and W. H. Hellen of Uniontown, E.C. Bald of the Bald Motor Company of Pittsburgh, O.E. Jackson of the Jackson Motor Supply Company in Pittsburgh, and E.M. Magnussen from the sales department of Detroit, Michigan's Hudson Motor Company. G. Carl Areford announced the start and finish of each contestant. Wallace Miller and R. Coller were the timers at the end of the course and George Holland of George Bailey's Jewelry Store kept time at the start. The race's referee was Frank Rosboro. Ewing and J. Searight Marshall kept score. F.S. Areford and J. Benton Crow officiated at the start. C.W.Johnson and J.H. Cronick classified the automobiles.

The Tri State Telephone Company saw to it that the officials at the start and the end of the course kept in constant communication. T.E.Lynn, manager at the Connellsville branch, would phone his boss, A.M. Critchton, when a car took off, informing those at the end of the track of the car's number and time. When the car topped the mountain, Critchton in turn called officials at the start and relayed the driver's times so that all could keep up with who was in what position in the race.

A Free-For-All event was held and then events A through H and exhibitions by local dealers who were not permitted to enter the race. In the Free-

For-All, Ed Riffle drove his Packard to the top in 2 minutes and 2 seconds, winning the silver loving cup. The cup was donated by the Fayette County Automobile Association, and was to be competed for each year. Second place went to John H. Work, who drove his Pope-Hartford to the top in 2 minutes and 20 seconds. He also won a silver loving cup. Third place went to A.J. Hubert of South Brownsville, who won his loving cup with a time of 2 minutes and 33 seconds. W.T. Carroll came in fourth with a time of just one second behind Hubert, also winning a loving cup.

**Event A** – was for cars which cost under $1,000.00 A.J.Hulbert ran his Ford up the course in 2 minutes and 35 seconds to win his first prize: a set of casings. A.C. Johnson's Buick won him a set of tubes with a time of 2 minutes and 54 seconds. Dr. A.J. McHugh won a silver loving cup as third prize when he topped the Summit at 3 minutes 5 seconds in his Hupmobile.

**Event B** – was held for cars ranging in price from $1,001.00 to $1,300.00. First place was nabbed by W.T.Carroll and his Buick with a time of 2 minutes and 28 seconds which won him a set of casings. Dr. A.E. Crow was 12 seconds behind his opponent which won him a set of tubes. Dr. J.A. Robinson won a loving cup for his third place time of 2 minutes and 53 seconds in his Buick.

**Event C** – for cars costing from $1,301.00 to $1,600.00. Mr.. Cramer won his set of casings driving a Correja in 2 minutes and 30 seconds. Sheriff M.A. Kiefer's Buick took the hill at 2 minutes and 59 seconds winning him a set of tubes.

**Event D** – had one entry whose Buick car was from $1,600.00 to $2,000.00 in price. O.P. Powell's time was 3 minutes 10 seconds.

**Event E** – These cars cost from $2,000.00 to $2,750.00. The first prize went to C.D. Bortz whose Kline car marked a time of 2 minutes 7 seconds. John G. Gibbs was 40 seconds behind in his Mitchell.

**Event F** – Only one car entered the $2,751.00 to $3,750.00 category. R.W. Playford, Esq. did the hill in 2 minutes and 36 seconds.

**Event G** – For cars costing $3,751.00 to $4,500.00, W.C. Gan's Packard won the casings with 2 minutes 13 seconds. G.S. Harah's Packard brought up the rear 19 seconds later.

**Event H** – was for cars costing over $4,500.00. Howell McCormick beat all event times by winning the casings and an automobile fire extinguisher with a time of 1 minute and 55 seconds in his $5,000.00 Packard. Ed Riffle took the set of tubes right behind McCormick.

John Hogsett won the booby prize for the worst time in all the events for his time in Event A. He was awarded a pocket lapel flexible cord searchlight for his Buick's efforts of 4 minutes 13 seconds.

During the Dealers Exhibitions, Keystone Garage manager, Fred Close, beat all the events times when he and Chauncey Harader took a Stoddard-Dayton car to the top in 1 minute 49 seconds. Tri State Garage's John Shaw came close in his Ford with a time of 1 minute 56 seconds.

After the race, traffic was backed up when the Johnson Brewery truck caught fire at the foot of the mountain with the following men riding in it: Orville Johnson, Robert Henry, Joe Kolmer, Christopher Welsh, Charles Hurley, Dan Murphey, Frank Roberts, Ewing Baker (driver), Bert Brooke, John Humphreys, and Earl Johnson. It seems that the connection on the gas tank of the big Packard broke and when Baker reached the foot of the hill, the vehicle backfired and caught fire. The truck was decorated with flags and an awning which lent fuel to the fire as did the 25 gallons of gasoline and load of wood they were carrying. The loss totaled $1,000.00 as it was not insured.

The first annual race was considered a success and plans began immediately for a larger one the next year.

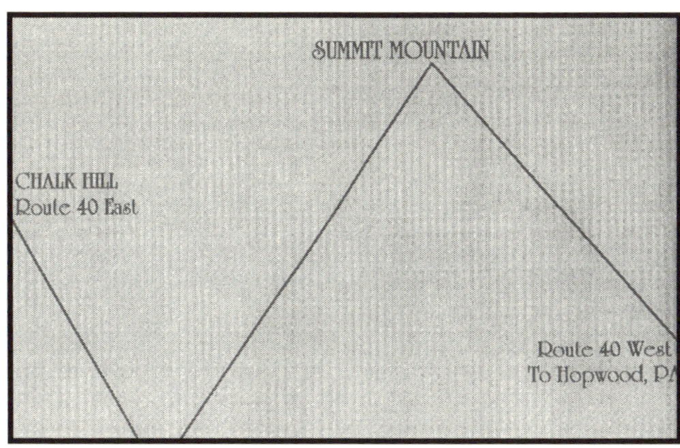

Summit Mountain Hill Climb 1913 – 1915. The Mountain Water Club was home of the famous watering trough that has saved the life of many an animal and motor vehicle traveling Summit Mountain's steep grade. The men at the long table are part of the officials working one of the Summit Mountain Hill Climbs. This crowd seems to be enjoying the show. On the right side of the lower porch stands George Flavius Titlow (hatless). A man in the group at the edge of the woods raises his drink in a toast. Are they guarding the still I have heard about?

# Official Program

## SECOND ANNUAL HILL CLIMB

## AUTOMOBILE CLUB OF FAYETTE COUNTY, PA.

ON THE NATIONAL PIKE

FROM HOPWOOD TO THE SUMMIT OF CHESNUT RIDGE

DISTANCE, 3 MILES--15840 FEET

**JUNE 17, 1914**

Amateur Events limited to members of the Automobile Club of Fayette County, Pa.

**JUNE 18, 1914**

Professional Events under the rules and with the sanction of the Contest Board of the American Automobile Association, sanction grant No. 663.

AND

Under the rules and with the sanction of the Federation of American Motorcyclists, sanction grant No. 2248.

**COMMITTEE IN CHARGE**

F. H. Rosboro, Chairman; C. W. Johnson, F. A. Close, J. H. Cronick, F. B. Hess, John C. Shaw, Dr. A. C. Smith, E. Gadd Snider.

PRICE, 10 CENTS

RECORD PRESS UNIONTOWN, PA.

## THE AUTOMOBILE CLUB OF FAYETTE COUNTY

FIRST NATIONAL BANK BUILDING,

UNIONTOWN, PA.

### OFFICERS.

John M. Core.......... President
R. W. Playford.......... Vice President
George L. Armstrong.......... Vice President
George F. Titlow.......... Vice President
H. B. Moore.......... Vice President
George J. Edel.......... Vice President
J. Searight Marshall.......... Secretary
F. H. Rosboro.......... Treasurer

### BOARD OF GOVERNORS.

G. S. Harah, F. H. Rosboro, H. R. Sackett
R. E. Umbel, A. P. Austin, George Whyel
Chas. S. Hempstead, S. E. Taylor, C. F. Eggers
A. J. Cochran, J. B. Wood, F. M. Semans, Jr.
C. W. Johnson, M. A. Kiefer, W. L. Graham

### MEMBERSHIP COMMITTEE.

Earl S. Areford, George J. Edel, A. D. Soisson
Paul D. Howard, George L. Armstrong, Charles Mathiot
Wallace Miller, George M. Rathmell, Clarke M. Chisholm
Dr. A. S. Hagan

### HIGHWAYS COMMITTEE.

George Whyel, T. Scott Dunn, Charles F. Eggers
J. L. Cochran, C. L. Snowden, W. L. Graham
Alva M. Walters, H. R. Sackett, M. M. Cochran
C. E. Lenhart

### LEGISLATION AND LITIGATION.

W. E. Crow, R. W. Playford, J. M. Core

### HOUSE COMMITTEE.

A. P. Austin, R. E. Umbel, F. M. Semans, Jr.

### ENTERTAINMENT COMMITTTEE.

George F. Titlow, G. S. Harah, R. E. Umbel

### GRIEVANCE COMMITTEE.

John T. Robinson, W. A. Stone, W. C. Black
E. B. Marshall, B. B. Howell

### AUDITING COMMITTEE.

M. H. Bowman, Charles T. Cramer, W. C. Black

### PUBLICITY COMMITTEE.

P. A. Johns, Marl A. Kiefer, W. E. Crow, C. O. Schroyer

# *The Second Annual Summit Mountain Hill Climb – 1914*

On Wednesday June 17, 1914, the *Morning Herald's* Coiley S. Baker described the second annual Summit Mountain Hill Climb as "the greatest automobile racing meet ever held in Pennsylvania." Uniontown and the mountain were filed with visitors there to witness the amateur events and the Summit was closed to traffic at 1 o'clock in the afternoon. "There is an air of subdued anxiety throughout the town," the newspaper said the day before the races. "The talk is entirely of the races. Long into last night could be heard the chug of the powerful racing machines as they were being tested out in the local garages, or taken out across the mountain road." A Mr.. Reisinger of Shaw Motors lent his Ford to the *Herald* newspaper staff for their use so the races could be covered in detailed accounts during this two-day contest.

The line-up for Wednesday, June 17, 1914 went like this:

First Event

*Amateur Motorcycle racing under rules of the Federation of American Motorcyclists.*

Second Event

*Stock cars selling for $1600.00 and less.*

| Owner/Driver | Car |
|---|---|
| 1. H.C. Brock | Buick Roadster |
| 2. Max Hannen | Buick Roadster |
| 3. W.T. Carroll | Buick Touring |
| 4. A.E. Crow | E.M.F. Runabout |
| 5. C.E. Wooding | Buick Roadster |
| 6. C.H. Cramer | Correja Roadster |
| 7. Kerfoot W. Daly | Buick Roadster8. |
| A.J. Hulbert | Ford Roadster |

Third Event

*Stock Cars selling at $1,601.00 to $3,000.00*

| | |
|---|---|
| 1. E. Gadd Snider | Mercer Touring |
| 2. Wallace Miller | Hudson Roadster3. |
| R.C. Bigler | Mercer Raceabout |
| 4. H.R. Sackett | Buick Roadster |
| 5. J. Philip Roman | Haynes Touring |
| 6. O.P. Powell | Buick Roadster |

Fourth Event

*Stock Cars selling at $3,000.00 and over*

| | |
|---|---|
| 1. F.M. Seamans, Jr. | Pierce Arrow Touring |
| 2. R.F. Playford | Lozier Roadster |
| 3. George Whyel | Peerless Touring |
| 4. Arthur C. Smith | Mercedes Roadster |
| 5. M. Aaron | Lozier Touring |

Fifth Event

*Special Event for cars entered in above events.*

| | |
|---|---|
| 1. C.E. Wooding | Buick Roadster |
| 2. C.H. Cramer | Correja Roadster |
| 3. Kerfoot W. Daly | Buick Roadster |
| 4. A.J. Hulbert | Ford Roadster |
| 5. R.C. Bigler | Mercer Raceabout |
| 6. H.R. Sackett | Buick Roadster |
| 7. J. Philip Roman | Haynes Touring |
| 8. O.P. Powell | Buick Touring |
| 9. M. Aaron | Lozier Touring |

*Cars are listed in the order in which they started.*

## Accept Our Thanks

The Boys' Brigade, in full uniform, will assist the other sworn officers in patrolling the course during each day's events.

One Red Cross Hospital will be located at the upper watering trough in charge of Dr. A. E. Crow and two experienced nurses, and one will be located at the Turkey's Nest in charge of Dr. G. H. Robinson and two experienced nurses.

The First Aid team of the Boy Scouts will be located at the finish fully equipped to attend to any duties required of them.

The telephone and electrical timing devices were designed and furnished by the Tri-State Telephone Company, especially for these contests—and through the courtesy of the Postal Telegraph Company the wires and appliances are strung on their poles.

The stop watches used in the timing are Swiss (Guinand) Split Second Timers furnished by Cross & Beguelin, of New York City, through their local representative, T. L. Collier.

Six members of the First Aid team of Oliver No. 1 will be located at the Upper Watering Trough on the 27th and at the Turkey's Nest on the 28th. Six members of the Continental No. 1 First Aid team will be located at the Turkey's Nest on the 27th and at the Upper Watering Trough on the 28th. Stations will have full equipment to take care of any work required of them.

## Prizes in Amateur Events Were Donated By the Following Firms:

FIRST PRIZE—4 Vacuum Cup Casings
By the Pennsylvania Rubber Company through Wright-Metzler Company.

FIRST PRIZE—4 Nobby Tread Casings
By the U. S. Tire Company through Pittsburgh Agency.

FIRST PRIZE—4 Non-Skid Casings
By the Firestone Tire Company through Jackson Motor Supply Company.

SECOND PRIZE—2 Pa. Vacuum Cup Rear Casings
By the Automobile Club of Fayette County.

SECOND PRIZE—2 G. & J. Non-Skid Rear Casings
By the Automobile Club of Fayette County.

SECOND PRIZE—2 Firestone Rear Casings
By the Automobile Club of Fayette County.

THIRD PRIZES—2 Firestone Inner Tubes, 2 G. & J. Inner Tubes and 2 Pa. Inner Tubes
By the Automobile Club of Fayette County.

Event No. 5, First Prize Cup donated by the Automobile Club of Fayette County, Pa., won last year by E. H. Riffle.

Fourth Prize in Events 2, 3 and 4, Pyrene Extinguishers by the Manufacturers through Standard Auto Company.

Fourth Prize Motorcycle Event, 5 gallon Motorcycle oil by The A. D. Miller Sons Co., through J. J. Graham and E. J. Miller.

Fifth Prize in Events 2, 3 and 4 and Second Prize in Event No. 5, 5 gallon "R" Invincible Auto Oil by A. D. Miller Sons Co., through J. J. Graham and E. J. Miller.

The Summit Hotel was running at full capacity during the Summit Mountain Hill Climbs. Dr. Joseph Van Kirk passed on here after dropping over from excitement during the races. It was a hot and blistering day until late afternoon, when clouds passed over the sun giving drivers and spectators much needed relief. We must assume that the pool at the hotel was brimming with swimmers and the tavern and restaurant overflowing with thirsty customers. It was out front here where George Titlow's Peerless caught fire twice while parked during the races. A handy fire extinguisher saved the engine and protected nearby automobiles from the flames. One can imagine the view they had of the congested mountain – crowds and hot rods shaking the hill!

Motorcycle races were a big draw in the Summit Mountain Hill Climbs 1913-1915. Bikes like the Flying Merkle, Excelsior, Indian and Harley-Davidson flew up the ridge to the Summit Hotel. Unknown driver topping the Smmit Mountain after a grueling race.

# OFFICIALS FOR HILL CLIMB

## JUNE 17 AND 18, 1914

A. A. A. OFFICIAL REPRESENTATIVE.

P. D. Folwell.................................. Philadelphia, Pa.

F. A. M. OFFICIAL REPRESENTATIVE.

L. B. Fleming.................................. Pittsburgh, Pa.

REFEREE.

L. B. Fleming .................................. Pittsburgh, Pa.

STARTER.

Webb Jay.................................. Chicago, Ill.

ASSISTANT STARTERS.

J. H. Cronick.................................. Uniontown, Pa.
E. B. Marshall.................................. Uniontown, Pa.
Charles Saupp .................................. Pittsburgh, Pa.

JUDGES.

Charles M. Kelley.................................. Pittsburgh, Pa.
John M. Core.................................. Uniontown, Pa.
Richard Kennerdell.................................. Franklin, Pa.

DIRECTOR OF EVENTS.

Herne Nadall.................................. Chicago, Ill.

TIMERS.

Wallace Miller (or representative).................. Uniontown, Pa.
George M. Baily (or representative).................. Uniontown, Pa.
William Hunt (or representative).................. Uniontown, Pa.
Thomas Collier (or representative).................. Uniontown, Pa.

SCORERS.

J. Searight Marshall.................................. Uniontown, Pa.
D. M. Bryar .................................. Pittsburgh, Pa.
Earl S. Areford .................................. Uniontown, Pa.

TECHNICAL COMMITTEE.

J. C. Donahue.................................. Uniontown, Pa.
J. H. Cronick.................................. Uniontown, Pa.
A. E. Corns .................................. Uniontown, Pa.

# SCHEDULE OF AMATEUR EVENTS

## JUNE 17, 1914

These events are open only to members of the Automobile Club of Fayette County, Pa., and each car or motorcycle entered must be owned by a member of the club and driven either by the owner, or some member of the family, who is a member of the club and who comes under the qualification of an "Amateur."

### "STOCK CARS" PRICE CLASSIFICATION

A "stock car" entered in these events must be, or have been, a gasoline car on sale through all the regular selling representatives of the manufacturers during the period of its production; and must carry all the regular equipment ordinarily used by the owner, but top or windshield may be lowered or removed.

Each entrant will be allowed a flying start of 100 yards.

Robert Evans, a driver from Detroit, Michigan, wrote a column for the *Morning Herald* which appeared the day of the first race up the west side of Summit Mountain. Cars had been tested on the hill for several days as Fayette County Automobile Club officials provided many men along the course to assure the safety of drivers and spectators alike. On Wednesday June 17, 1914, Evans described the Summit Mountain as "the best hillclimbing course in the country." From the Barnes Estate in Hopwood to the top of the Summit, speed monsters were heating up the road, and for the most part, keeping their times to themselves. Charlie Johnson was picked to be the all-around favorite as he ran his Packard, Buick and Chandlier in daredevil fashion, wowing spectators with his cool judgement and iron nerve while hugging the rocks along Turkey's Nest Curve at breakneck speeds.

*The Morning Herald* headline read...

## *Turkey's Nest Scene of Thrills*
## *Four Racers Hurt*

H.R. Sackett, aged 55 of Smithfield, PA, was rounding the long sweeping curve on the Turkey's Nest Bridge during the free-for-all race, when the left front tire of his Buick Roadster blew out. He lost control of the vehicle. As Sackett realized he was about to crash he raised up on his feet and remained in the plunging car. He clutched the steering wheel with his right hand and tried to steer the wheel away from the cliff in a futile effort. Sackett leaned over in his seat and turned off the motor, bracing himself for the impact. He was bounced 5 feet into the air when he hit at about 45 miles per hour and members of the Continental 1 First Aid Team grasped him as he landed into the wrecked Buick. The ligaments of his left ankle were sprained from striking one of the foot brakes and his front fenders and wheels were demolished, but Sackett protested treatment and demanded a cane just minutes after entering the hospital tent. "Give me a cane. I want to see how it looks," he exclaimed. The paper described this incident as "a great display of nerve."

Roy Deck, 22, of Oliver, Pennsylvania acquired a laceration of the left leg while being thrown from his Indian motorcycle on the Turkey's Nest Bridge. R. L.Pixler of Morgantown, West Virginia was thrown head first from his Crawford motorcycle into this same cliff, suffering a bruise on the back of the head and a scraped left shoulder.

John C. Shaw of Shaw Motor Company, Uniontown, demolished his White car and was bruised and cut up from tangling with that mean Turkey's Nest Curve during the morning's tryouts. It is fair to assume that most spectators were packed around the curve that tossed racers about like they were toys.

There were two minor incidents reported in the *Pittsburgh Gazette Times*. Homer Mathis from Charleroi was the first racer up the mountain and the only motorcyclist who made it to the finish line. He first crashed into a telephone pole and was thrown a couple of yards. After remounting, he again lost control of his machine and tore through the wooden fence along the road. He had cut his legs and arms, but climbed back on and made it to the top of the three mile run. Max Hannen of Uniontown drove his Buick Roadster off course up the cliff and into the crowd, cutting his legs and hands. He backed the machine up and completed the race. George Titlow's Roadster was sitting at the Summit Inn where he and his family watched the race, when its engine caught fire and blazed for some time, threatening nearby machines.

Turkey's Nest Curve on Summit Mountain took its toll during the hill climbs, injuring many and killing J.E. Shafer of Pittsburgh. It was an "S" curve with a rocky cliff protruding on the bend just below the bridge. These rocks were a hazard to those who came near at a high rate of speed.

# *Event Winners*

R.C. Bigler made the best time of the day in his Mercer Raceabout climbing the 3 miles in 4 minutes and 42 and 2/5 seconds in the special events race. He won the silver loving cup, which must be won for 2 consecutive years in order to permanently retain it. E. H. Riffle gave it to Bigler, for he had won it in 1913. Many of the starters did not finish this race because of blowouts and accidents, but the following is a summary of the days events:

**Event 1** – Homer Mathis set a time of 4 minutes and 43 and 4/5 seconds on his Emblem motorcycle.

**Event 2** – W.T. Carroll set a time of 5 minutes and 23 3/5 seconds in his Buick touring car. H.C. Brooke was 18 seconds behind him in his Buick Roadster. Max Hannen took 3rd place with 6 minutes and 10 3/5 seconds.

**Event 3** – R.C. Bigler won in his Mercer at 4 minutes 45 seconds. H.R. Sackett made 2nd place with 5 minutes 35 2/3 seconds in his Buick. O.P Powell came in 9 seconds behind to take 3rd in his Buick.

**Event 4** – M. Aaron of Cleveland set a time of 5 minutes 25 seconds in his Lozier.

**Event 5** – R.C. Bigler came in 1st again with a time of 4 minutes 41 2/5 seconds. O.P. Powell came in 2nd with 5 minutes 45 4/5 seconds in his Buick and C.E. Wooding set a 3rd place time of 6 minutes 32 2/5 seconds.

That was it for the amateur races and it was decided this day that next years events would be for strictly professional drivers.

The days officials were: P.D. Folwell, AAA representative from Philadelphia and L.H. Flersing, F.A.M. representative and referee of the race. He was from Pittsburgh.

**Starters:** Web Jay of Chicago, Joseph H. Cronick, E.B. Marshall and Charles Saupp of Pittsburgh.

**Judges:** Charles M. Kelley of Pittsburgh, John M. Cire of Uniontown and Richard Kennerdell of Franklin.

**Director** of the race was Berne Nadall of Chicago.

**Scorers:** J.E. Wright Marshall of Uniontown, D.M. Bryon of Pittsburgh and E.S. Ford of Uniontown.

James Edward Shafer 34, of the Pittsburgh Mercer Car Company had his life taken from him by the Turkey's Nest Curve while returning to Hopwood from the Summit Mountain. He had just successfully completed the course in a practice run and was heading down the hill to line up for the race. The grim reaper had other ideas for him and Shafer died of a punctured lung.

# J.E. Shafer, Auto Racer, Dies of Hurts in Hospital; Dr. Jos. Van Kirk, of Elizabeth, Dead From Excitement

The headlines the next morning were clear. Accidents marred the hill climbs as crowds surged onto the road. Two men died. Six were injured and many narrow escapes occurred. By now, "Turkey's Nest" was called the "Death Curve."

At just a few minutes before the professional races got under way, James Edward Shafer was descending Summit Mountain to take his place in the first event line up in front of the Barnes Estate at the foot of the hill. There were several versions reported as to what actually happened depending on where the people were standing. Some thought he was overcome by heat and exhaustion as he had an earlier accident. At the second watering trough the day before, he broke the front axle and ran the Mercer into the Mountainside. He called Pittsburgh and had the part he needed sent to him. It is said that the morning of the second day of the races, Shafer did the work of three men getting his car ready to go by 2pm. He was weak and Charlie Johnson advised him to forego the test run. Some said they believed the driver misunderstood the red signal flag he was given at the bend. It meant all was clear, but he may have construed it to mean "danger ahead." The thought is that he stopped so suddenly the car flipped on its roof. Some say he waved to them as he passed on his fatal decline but then seemed to faint, his hand dropping and going limp. The car then, gradually, at about 15 mph, struck the culvert at Turkey's Nest, then turned "turtle" and threw Shafer under the rear. The Mercer then flipped to its wheels and left the driver face down in a puddle of the blood that gushed from his head.

Spectators started screaming for the physicians and first aid team who could not see the accident from where they were stationed on the other side of the high rocky curve. They did hear a bursting tire on that side of the bend, and some believe the blowout started the driver skidding. One man said the driver told him when he ran up to the car, that he thought the steering went. Whatever the case, Shafer was at first talking to folks telling them that he would be ready for the next race and this was announced. He was carried to the first aid tent and followed down the pike by hundreds of onlookers. Shafer was pale as death and suffering from his injuries. The car was severely damaged. The steering wheel was torn off and it is believed this caused his head injury. The fatal wound came when a hub flew off and hit him in the chest, breaking ribs and puncturing a lung. They say it took the entire strength of a man to release the brakes on the car as they were pressed so tightly to the floor. About 20 minutes after the accident, E.L. Cramer, a member of the first aid team, and George F. Titlow rushed Shafer to the Uniontown Hospital, as it was realized his injuries were indeed serious. During the ride to the hospital Titilow questioned Shafter about what had actually happened.

"I got in a little too fast," was his faint reply.

"Were you flagged?" Titlow asked.

"Yes," he mumbled in a low tone as his bleeding

Ed Shafer (center) poses with the Mercer at the Mercer garage in Pittsburgh, 1914, just before being killed at the Turkey's Nest Curve.

head dropped to Titlow's shoulder, staining his shirt. These were James Edward Shafer's last words. At 5:15pm that day he passed on.

Shafer had told his parents, Mr.. and Mrs. Ed E. Shafer of 9 Gaskel Street, Pittsburgh that he was going on a business trip. He worked for Mercer and they were shocked to get the news of their son's death by race car at death's curve. Shafer was a newlywed who left his new wife and eleven month old son behind. At the time of his death, Shafer owned extensive real estate in Pittsburgh and was an up and coming entrepreneur. He was a Mason and was buried in uniform at the Mt. Lebanon Cemetery. He was born July 21, 1879 in Whitehaven, Pennsylvania.

Thirty five minutes after Shafer expired, Dr. Jos. Van Kirk died at the Summit Hotel. During the first racing event of the day, Van Kirk was stricken with apoplexy (stroke) from the excitement and heat, and dropped to the pavement of the National Road. Dr. Neff failed to revive him and several other physicians joined to assist. This stopped the motorcycle races for half an hour until Dr. A. E. Crow came from the hospital tent and Van Kirk's chauffeur carried the 55 year old now-conscious man, into the Summit

Hotel. He immediately collapsed, struggled for two hours and never regained consciousness. He was an Elizabeth councilman.

In the second event J.D. Kerr ran into the crowd in his Kline car just across the pike from where Shafer lost his life. Davy Davies, 19, of Uniontown, was hit, fracturing his left leg and bruising his legs and arms. Kerr was traveling on the curve at 55 mph when he skidded on the Turkey's Nest Curve and into the crowd. He then righted himself and went on to clock the second best time made for the day: 3:57. An Indian motorcycle driven by Ewing Herrold made the fastest time of the day with 3:49; but this was before the races began.

During the test runs some better times were made than in the races. This was due to the enormous crowds (10,000!) that were gathered along the entire course, especially the Turkey's Nest Curve and the Mountain Water Club. Many drivers were afraid to hit someone and could not let their machines do their best because of this. According to the newspapers, drivers continually dodged spectators. Several of the races were run over again including Kerr's, because of the interference. The Boys Brigade was hired to keep people off of the course. This was not an easy job. They were armed with swords and bayonets and drew them when people insisted on crossing the road during and between the races. Crowds cheered the boys on when men cursed them for stopping their progress across the course.

This day Charlie Johnson had a blowout before the race as he descended the Summit. He hit the mountainside and was shaken, with head, arm and body bruises and lacerations. He was taken home, but returned to wow audiences with his nerve.

W.R. Scott of Waynesburg was tended to in the hospital tent after ramming the cliff at the Mountain Water Club and cutting his face and hands.

C.M. Williams was thrown from his car while making a trial record run up the hill. He cut his head and sprained his back.

Emmett Ball collided with H.C. Homer and was treated for cuts of the arms and body before the races began. I.N. Natcher was run down by a speeding car and had injuries over his body and head.

## *And the Winners Were...*

**Event 1** – J.M. Taylor won $100.00 when his Flying Merkle motorcycle took him to the top of the Summit in 3:50 4/5.

**Event 2** – John McGann of Boston won $150.00 in his Metz with a time of 4:00 3/5

### Our Object

The Automobile Club of Fayette County was organized not only for the benefit of its members, but in a much broader sense to do everything possible at all times for the best interests of the people of this section and to see that Fayette County is always on the map. We now have 350 of the county's best citizens enrolled as members of the Club with a number of like citizens of our adjoining counties. We expect to have 1,000 members in the near future and would be glad to have you join a live organization that will at all times stand for the best interests of Western Pennsylvania in the good roads movement and whatever seems to be best for the people.

**Event 3** – C.W. Johnson won $225.00 in his Buick for a time of 3:58 3/5

**Event 4** – I.P Fetterman of Pittsburgh won $300.00 for a time of 4:09 in a 90hp Simplex.

**Event 5** – J.D. Kerr set a time of 3:57 4/5 in his Kline for a First Place prize of $300.00.

Kerr set his winning time after rerunning the track. He had earlier complained (after being forced to hit someone with his car) that there was barely room for the car to fit through the throngs of people. He then beat Johnson's time by just under a minute. Several others ran the race a second time, but did not beat the winners. There was talk that Fetterman set a time of 3:20 in the free-for-all, but the timing device did not credit him. The automatic timers used were called a "joke" by Robert Evans who said, "I believe the course has never before been covered in less time than Fetterman's."

The Summit Mountain Hill Climbs of 1914 & 1915 had their starting line in front of the Barnes Estate at the foot of Summit Mountain. These photos show the mansion, gazebo, bridge, and a group of grounds workers, who no doubt had a front row seat to the excitement of the races

# George Titlow Scores AAA Signal System

After the races, in a meeting at the Titlow Hotel, Mr.. Titlow blamed the AAA and not the Fayette Automobile Club for Shafer's death.

He was asked by a reporter, "Do you believe that Mr.. Shafer misunderstood the red flag that was given him at the curve to mean danger and stopped so suddenly as to overturn his car?"

To that he replied:

"Absolutely so. The red flag means danger everywhere we see it. Why should we allow the AAA or any other association come to Fayette County and tell us something that is against the laws of Pennsylvania and against the common practice? It is most absurd for a red flag on the National Pike to mean a clear track and only a short distance away at a railway crossing to have just the opposite meaning. In private race courses that may be alright. But on the National Pike, the common practice and and laws of our commonwealth, which teach us that red means danger, should be upheld. The AAA, in making a rule that red means a clear track and not danger does not comply with the law of the state of Pennsylvania and therefore should be changed and I am going to do all in my power to have it changed even if I have to go to the courts to do it. The AAA has no right to change the law and endanger the public. Red means danger everywhere and that should be observed on a race course the same as any other place. The AAA rules conflict with those of the commonwealth and I as Vice President of the Auto Club of Fayette County, am going to do my best to have them changed.

When Shafter came down the mountain yesterday, the red flag was flashed at the curb and he interpreted it to mean danger ahead and it was then that he threw on his brake and ran into the culvert and overturned his car. Had the proper signals been given according to the laws of the state and according to common practice instead of AAA rules, the accident would never have happened."

Charlie Johnson took exception to Titlow's statement as Titlow, John M. Core and F.H. Rosboro had a heated argument. It was decided that this would be taken up at the next meeting of the auto club.

The races this day ended around 6pm. This was just after Shafer and Van Kirk passed away. Can you imagine how Mr.. Titlow felt after being the last man to speak with Shafer as the driver fell limp on him. Titlow held the man all the way to the hospital.

In the meantime, J.D. Kerr, who broke Davy Davie's leg in a skid at Turkey's Nest Curve, stated that his car seemed to run around the boy before catching him with the rear right wheel. Kerr visited the victim the morning after the races and promised to do what he could for him.

After the races, Hopwood, Uniontown and the Summit were hopping with celebrations. Banners adorned cars and stretched across the pike asking drivers to drive at 15 mph during this congested time.

The papers said, "Not in years has such an army of humanity passed through our limits."

The drivers that everyone expected to win these races did not. Both Robert Evans and Charlie Johnson had suspicious engine trouble as did Mr.. Poffenberger. It was believed that someone tampered with their machines to keep them from winning. Because of this and discontent over the timing device used, I.P. Fetterman, Johnson, Poffenberger and C.E. Giddings put up $500.00 each to go to a Fourth of July race.

"My time will be considerably less than 4 minutes. I am willing to bet on it," Fetterman told the crowd at a meeting held at the Titlow Hotel a few days after the races. The holiday race was nixed by the State Highway Department because "pleasure seekers, holiday parties and tourists of all kinds should not be hindered from their destinations." Johnson joked that he would hold the race and pay the fine, but in the end complied with the law.

Mr. George F. Titlow was the man who first brought automobiles to Uniontown. He was in charge of entertainment for the Automobile Club of Fayette County who held the races.

Charlie Johnson was at this time the best local driver around.

# *Ralph DePalma Bows to Local Speed King*

In 1915, Ralph DePalma won the Indianapolis"500" race, but he could not beat Uniontown's own Charlie Johnson to the top of Summit Mountain. Johnson had just been voted President of the new Uniontown Motoring Association which was incorporated just four days before this race. R.M. Campbell was Vice President, F.A. Close, Secretary and H.D. Hutchison, Treasurer. A charter was granted in Harrisburg and the club capitalized with $5,000.00. They lined up an all-professional race as the Summit Mountain was now known nationally as a formidable climb. Entries poured in days before the races and drivers from many states had their cars sent here by railway. The judges stand was erected and an improved timing device installed. As telegrams arrived from famous drivers from around the country, these were announced and the townspeople prepared for the excitement.

Three days before the race, Fred Close, manager of the Keystone Automobile Company of Uniontown, ran his Chalmers into a telephone pole just above the Barnes Estate in order to avoid hitting a car driven by Roy Stentz. The pole was broken in two places and the car, badly damaged. When Close was brought home by Dr. Crow, his wife collapsed of fright and was taken to the hospital where she spent two days recovering from nervous shock. The Chalmers was repaired in time for the races.

Ralph DePalma and Joe Dawson (1912 Indy Winner) ran into each other the night before the races at the Gallatin Hotel where Ralph said, "Hello, Joe. What are you doing here? If I had known you were here, I would never have come down."

## *The Third Annual Summit Mountain Hill Climb June 24, 1915 – Official Program of Day's Races:*

**Event 1** Motorcycles:
1. Excelsor – Bob Perry
2. Excelsor – Carl Goudy
3. Thor – W. Carl Bentz
4. Indian
5. Indian
6. Merkle – Maldwyn Jones
7. Harley Davidson
8. Harley Davidson

**Event 2** Cars
1. Chalmers – A.E. Walden
2. Buick – A.D. Spenser
3. Maxwell – C.M. Hansel
4. Ford – Guy Woodward
5. Ford – Ollie Lemon
6. Sazon – M.A. Crocker
7. Metz – D.W. Hickey
8. Hispano – Ralph DePalma
9. Morse Cycle – E. Beequeet

**Event 3** Free-For-All
1. Overland – T.S. O'Rourke
2. Dickinson Special – J.W. Dickinson
3. Hispana Suiza – Joseph Boyer
4. Isotta – James Benedict
5. Simplex – I.P. Fetterman
6. Beaver Bullet – G.B. Gardner
7. Darracq Special – C.M. Williams

8. Buick 16 – Roy Stenz
9. Haynes – Alva Hughson
10. Mercer – J.J. Ryan
11. Mercedes – T.P. Rose
12. Mercer – A. Pehrson
13. Packard – C.W. Johnson
14. Lozier – H.E. Cupps
15. Fiat Special – Ben Hill
16. Chalmers – A.E. Walden
17. Haynes – F.M. Seanor
18. Buick – A.D. Spenser
19. Marmon – J. Dawson
20. Mercedes Special – Ralph DePalma

# *Charlie Johnson Wins Hill Climb Honor in 3:27 2-5 Not an Accident Mars Third Annual Summit Event*

The estimated crowd for the third annual Summit Mountain Hill Climb, Thursday, June 24, 1915, was 25,000. The three mile course was jammed with spectators, but for once there were no accidents. In his Packard Greyhound, Charlie Johnson set a record for the course and beat the champion speed king of the world, Ralph DePalma. Johnson was the favorite in the race to win. He knew every inch of the road and DePalma only had a few test drives under his belt. The paper stated that "with Charlie and his car and the road such intimate friends the result of the race was almost inevitable. Many predicted that Johnson would be killed in the race because he was number 13, but he won and became the most talked-about man in town. DePalma came in sixth place with a time of 3:55 2-5 in the Mercedes Special. Joe Dawson did not drive in the race and neither did D.W. Hickey who hurt his hand the day before and could not drive his Metz. DePalma won a prize of $50.00 for his sixth place in the Free-For-All.

Afterwards, DePalma told Johnson, "You got the victory this year, Charlie, and you can keep it till next year. Then I'm coming down here and taking it away from you."

They say DePalma laughed at the way he was invited to Uniontown by Johnson, and then beaten by him. "It's the best list of entries I ever competed against in a hill climb," he said. "The course is everything. You must know those curves. A few times over it is not enough. But the way that Johnson went over it can not be beaten. It was the finest exhibition of mountain racing I ever saw. And it is certainly credible to the participants as well as to the winners. And the way they took care of the entrants and visitors can not be improved upon. Uniontown is sure one live burgh. Its drivers and auto men have the ginger. But where did all those cars come from? Thank everybody for the swell way in which I was treated and tell them that I'll be back next year."

DePalma was the star attraction at the races. Many did not believe he was coming until they saw for themselves. He showed, but almost did not race when he broke his magneto shaft the day before the races on a test run up the hill. The part was rushed from Pittsburgh by Mr.. Russell of the Packard Motor Car Company. The Standard Garage turned their place over to the speed king and his car was ready for the race.

"Nothing could be more delightful than the visit and I am coming back next year with every first class driver in the country. Then I'm going to beat Johnson if I have to buy a Packard to do it," he said.

A Mr.. Charles Balsley filmed the races and the Lyric Theatre showed the movies to the crowds after the climb. Balsley filmed every race car at the Turkey's Nest Curve. While the new film was being developed, the movie from the 1914 hill climb was shown to the public for two days so spectators could refresh their memories about the races of the year before.

## *The winners of the races were:*

**Event 1** – Irving E. Janke; Harley Davidson Time – 3:16 1-5

**Event 2** – A.E. Walden; Chalmers Time – 3:50

**Event 3** – C.W. Johnson; Packard Time 3:37 2-5

"Ready for the opening race, December 2, 1916."

Uniontown Speedway boardtrack opening race December 2, 1916. The sixth and seventh men from the left are Gaston Weigle and Frank Galvin. They died shortly after this photograph was taken in a freak accident. Milton F. McBride is in the Olsen suit to Galvin's right. Two men to his right is Otto Henning. The next four are unknown. Smiling Ralph Mulford, Charlie Johnson (in suit), Ralph DePalma (knickers) with hands on shoulders of his mechanic, Louis Fountaine. John DePalma stands behind Fountaine's shoulder. Next is Tom Rooney. Two unknown. Hughie Hughes sits on wheel of car. He died later that day. To his right are Louis Chevrolet and Art Klein with Rosco Searles looking over Klein's shoulder. Man leaning against Peerless to the right is I.P. Fetterman. The press stand, to the right in this picture, was destroyed during this race.

Crowds gather for the opening race as Mr. Croft (inset) of Uniontown, prepares to photograph the drivers.

1916 Uniontown Speedway Opening Race Program Cover.

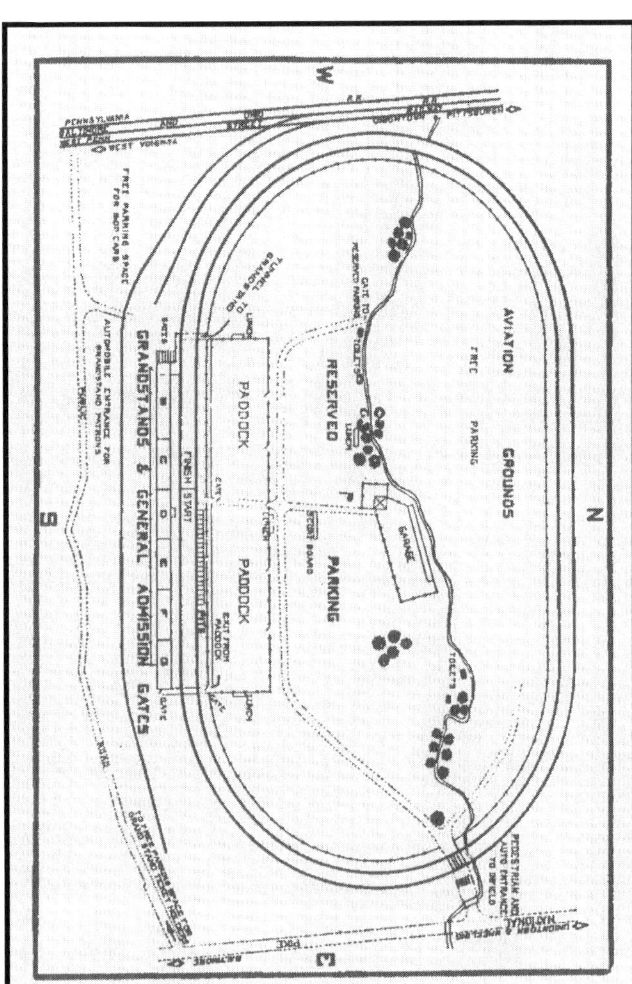


Uniontown Speedway Track Diagram.

Jack Prince, track designer, oversees his crew while they try to beat the clock and finish the Uniontown Speedway boardtrack by Thanksgiving of 1916.

The irony here is that they used horse drawn wagons to haul the lumber to build one of the most renowned wooden automobile racetracks in the world. Hopwood, 1916.

The Uniontown Speedway and grand stand are shown under construction to the right. Empty lumber wagons sit abandoned in the meadow where livestock roamed only a few weeks earlier.

Most of the speed demons had their race cars hauled in by special trains. Can you imagine driving these on wood at upwards of 100mph?

# *Yesteryear at the Uniontown Speedway 1916*

Just five days prior to the 1916 fourth annual Summit Mountain Hill Climb, the Pennsylvania State Highway Department banned racing on the mountain. Charles Johnson, Uniontown Buick dealer and the man who held the record time set for climbing the hill, took his post as President of the Uniontown Motoring Association seriously. This was a time when steel, coal, and coke had made many men rich as World War 1 was going on in Europe. Johnson solicited local barons and merchants, collecting $100,000.00 to build a wooden race track in Hopwood. He had been to races at the board track in Sheepshead Bay, New York and knew Uniontown had to have one for its own.

John C. "Jack" Prince was brought in. From 1881 to 1884 Prince was the champion cyclist of Europe. He then came to America where he won the world title, by beating all competition for two years from Boston to San Francisco. He moved to Omaha, Nebraska in 1886 and held races at the Exposition building on Capital Avenue where world famous cyclists such as Dingle, Shock, Knapp, Martin, Reading, and Morton competed. In 1887, he built a Coliseum on Lake and 20th Streets. It was considered the best ten-lap bicycle track in all the world.

At the Coliseum, he held an array of events in addition to professional bicycle races. These caused a great stir and filled the arena beyond capacity. He held an international tug-of-war that went on for nine consecutive evenings, matches between horses and bikes, wolf chases, and the grand opera. There was a skating rink. Billy Muldoon the champion wrestler, and even Jack Dempsey fought in Prince's palace. He promoted and organized the first exposition that was ever held in the city. This packed the place for two weeks.

Prince went on to build bicycle tracks around the country and after automobiles became the rage, he was commissioned to design and supervise the construction of wooden race tracks across America.

Johnson contacted the famous man and hired him to build a 1 and 1/8 mile oval track and a grand stand that would hold 20,000 fans, in the meadow on the southern side of the National Road at the west end of Hopwood, Pennsylvania. He gave the builder a three month deadline and Prince assured the Uniontown hot shot that he was up to the challenge.

They built the board track of 2 by 4's with a 100 man crew working long hours to meet their deadline. America was not yet in the fighting in Europe, but the Germans had torpedoed the British liner Lusitania, killing 139 Americans and the armed forces were preparing for war. This made workers difficult to find, so many high school boys pitched in after school. Lumber was hauled on horse drawn wagons as the transition from horse and buggy to

John F. (Jack) Prince

automobile was a slow one for the average family. The two forms of transportation co-existed for decades before the one car family became the norm.

Johnson realized his request to have the track completed for a Thanksgiving race would take a miracle. In the program for the opening race they stated that "The construction of the U.S.A. planked speedway will go down in the annals of history as an accomplishment that in retrospective view shows has never been equaled." They went on to say that board tracks take millions of feet of lumber of special grade and quality which made filling the order a slow and tedious process. During normal times it would have taken at least six months to deliver the lumber. With the war going on, they explain that it would take at least nine months if the lumber mills would accept such a large order at all. These companies were working at top speed already. Because one of the members of the American Lumber Company of Pittsburgh "had a great interest" in the speedway, Johnson succeeded in doing what many said could not be done. The Uniontown Speedway Association's board of directors conceded that "to him (Johnson) and him alone is due the honor, the praise, and the glory of achieving that which even the most optimistic of us said could not be accomplished."

On August 21, 1916 the property for the speedway was surveyed. Two days later the ground lease was attested. At this time there were cows, sheep, horses, and their young grazing lazily in the meadow; innocent of the tremendous noises that would soon fill the air. The first day of September saw the first stake driven. On September 8 the lumber order was placed with the American Lumber Company. One week later the first of the boards were delivered to Hopwood. The first

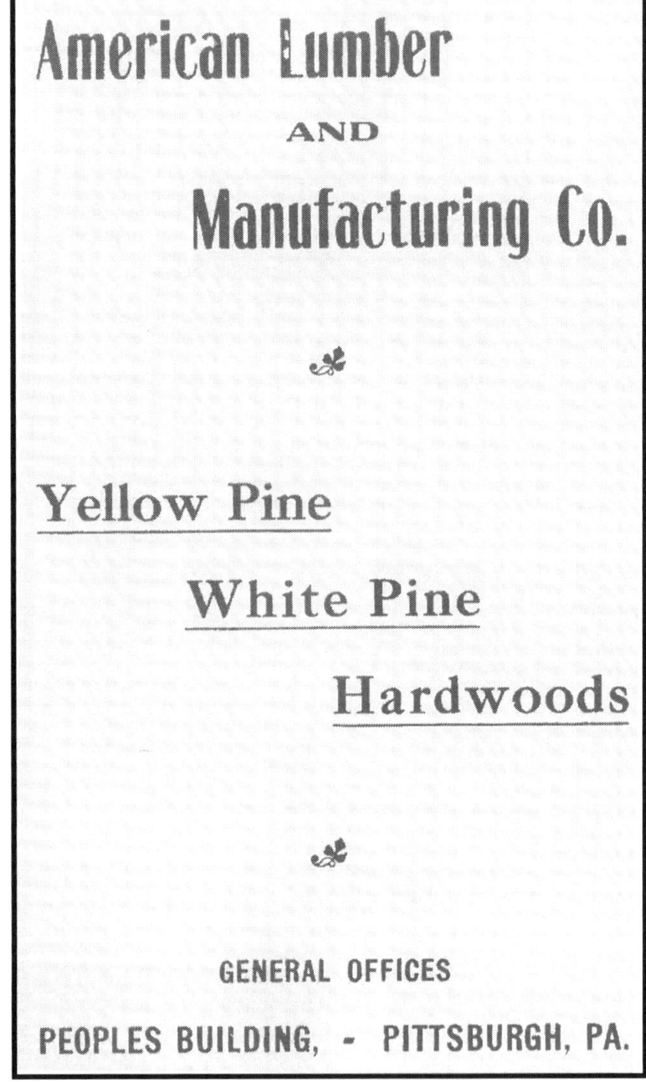

supporting timber was raised on the eighteenth. By November 1 they were laying surface plank. On the 21st of that month Barney Newgard's Crawford became the first car to be admitted to the track. Three days later the boxes were begun and the next day the track's wooden surface was completed. They laid 2 by 4's flat against each other to form the strong wooden floor. Because of the size of the natural amphitheatre in the meadow the track was a 1 and 1/8 mile oval. At 100mph, a lap was made at 40.50 seconds. It was written that a speed of 100mph on a board track was less dangerous than going 50mph on a flat dirt track.

The management of the Uniontown Speedway, in addition to Johnson being President and General Manager were as follows: First Vice President, Frank D. Saupp; Secretary, A.M. Hustead; Treasurer, Wendell A. Stone.

The officials were: Chairman of the Contest Board, Richard Kennerdell of New York; Representative of the Contest Board, F.H. Rosboro of Uniontown; Technical Committee Chairman, W.R. Strickler of Cleveland; Referee, Frank Rosboro of Uniontown; Starter, Webb Jay of Chicago; Assistant Starter, Jno. L. Cadwalader of Pittsburgh; Director of Timing, A.M. Crichton of Uniontown; Assistant Dir. of Timing, Wallace Miller of Uniontown; Director of Scoring, E.E. Porter of Uniontown; Clerk of Course, Don Beamer, Uniontown; Speed Reporter, Homer Burchinal of Uniontown.

The judges were: John J. Bell and C. E. Jackson of Pittsburgh.

Track doctors were C.M. Luman, E.H. Rebok, A.S. Hagan, snd Dr. Jackson.

Technical Committee members were John C. Donahue, Jos. Cronick, and Bert Abel.

Manager of Publicity was Ed F. Korbel of New York City.

Manager of Events was Neil Whalen from New York City.

Chairman of the Press was George B. Smith of Uniontown.

Scoreboard Manager was W.R. Smith of Connellsville.

Concession Committee members were R.S. Cook, H. Keller, Amadee Hagan, and Zed Francis.

Manager of Pyrotechnics was A. Bufano of Dunbar.

Telegraph service was provided by the Western Union and Postal Telegraph.

Tri-State Telephone set up and conducted telephone communications.

In a note from the speedway management in the program they described their maiden race this way:

Neil Whalen, Manager of Events

"We have brought here for your entertainment, the world's rising stars. Men and mounts who hold numerous world records. Men to whom fear is an unknown quantity and yet whose nerves have been tried in many prior contests. Men who could tell you of many harrowing moments, when a fraction of a second determined life or death for them and the destruction of their cars. Men whose vocation requires clean living. Men who follow the straight and narrow path possibly more closely than the exponents of any other line of sport. Men whom it is a pleasure to mingle and associate with, whose education and intelligence is considerably above the average, many of whom are graduates of the leading colleges of this and other countries. The rapid development of the pleasure car is due entirely to the research and mechanical knowledge of the racing driver."

Neil Whalen, Manager of Events, first drove a Matheson at Lowell, Mass in 1908. He did not win that race because a fly got in his carburetor and he lost time looking for flypaper to snag it! He won many of the "twice around the clock" grinds for the next year and in October 1909 he won the New York to Atlanta road race, covering 1063 miles in 54 hours and 15 minutes. The next year he won 10 of the 11 hill climbs he entered losing only to Ralph DePalma in Wilkes-Barre.

In 1912 Whalen upset his Case race car during the Indy 500 when an outside wheel came off. The car rolled and rolled but neither man was hurt. Days before the opening race in Uniontown Whalen said, "Thanksgiving Day the People of Uniontown will have something to be really-truly thankful for." At this time Harry Miller of L.A. was building Whalen the "U.S.A. Special". Whalen would represent the U.S.A. Speedway at all the big events around the circuit in this 165hp racer.

E.F. Corbel and M.W. Colwell were New York's number one promoters. They were hired to direct publicity for this and other major racing events around the country.

## *How Ill Fated National Team Came to Death*

Just two minutes after the Uniontown Speedway opened for its initial practice runs on Monday November 27, 1916, Frank Bush laughed and kissed his partner Charlie Heist's (driving) cheek and yelled, "We're off!" They were traveling over 60mph when coming around the steep back curve. The rear right tire blew as they came within two feet of the top of the embankment. Five hundred spectators watched as the car shot up and almost went over the back of the track. When the car crashed it rolled twice breaking through the guard rails and spinning forward. It then swerved back to the track, mowed down more of the railing and finally came to a stop after dragging along the bottom of the track. Bush was lifeless when the crowds approached the wreck and track doctors placed Heist on two planks to transport him to a car and then to the Uniontown Hospital. He never regained consciousness and was badly mashed as was Bush.

The team had been traveling together for a year racing on dirt tracks. They had been chosen by Pete Galanot, who ran a string of National race cars, for the National Motor Car Company of Pittsburgh, to go for the W.D. Johnston trophy in the dealer's race. Both men had raced at Indianapolis in addition to many state fairs and tracks around the country. After the second man died at 5:15pm that evening, their employer said, "Both of the boys are personal friends of mine, and I regret their death more than I can say. They drove my cars in almost every meet in which we have participated this year and I considered them to be the most conservative and careful drivers of the many who handled my cars. I have followed the racing game for the last five years, but you can say for me now that I am through. I want no more of it. The National car was one of the best equipped of any put on the track, and fate which proved unkind to that car can play the same trick with any other."

Heist's mother resided in Los Angeles, California and Bush's parents lived in Richmond, Virginia.

The following is the list of entries for the first event; Class E Non Stock. 300 cu. in. piston displacement, or under. Maximum weight 2500 pounds, 100 laps, 112 1/2 miles:

| ***Driver*** | ***Mechanic*** | ***Car*** |
|---|---|---|
| Ralph DePalma | Louis Fountaine | Mercedes |
| Dave Lewis | J. McAllister | Premier |
| Frank Galvin | Gaston Weigle | Premier |
| Barney Newgard | Emeret N. Pala | Crawford |
| Arthur H. Klein | E.J. Longchamps | Crawford |
| Hughie Hughes | | Hoskins |
| John DePalma | Billy Darragh | J.J.R. Special |
| M.F. McBride | George Baldini | Olsen |
| Bert Watson | William Claus | Olsen |
| James R. Meyer | George Downs | Pugh Special |
| Otto Henning | | Ogren Special |
| Louis Chevrolet | R.C. Searles | Frontenac |
| H.L. Robinson | | Haynes |
| Jack Conway | George J. Halley | Haynes |
| George Adams | | Adams Special |
| J. Mason | | Ogren |

The following is the list of entries for the second event - Class D, Non Stock. Free-For-All. For dealers residing within 150 miles of Uniontown, PA: 48 laps, 54 miles. The drivers and mechanics had to be from the specified area and the cars from the dealer's factory. The automobiles could be stripped and fitted with gears, timed, and tuned at the dealer's discretion:

| ***Driver*** | ***Mechanic*** | ***Car*** |
|---|---|---|
| Fred McCarthy | Charles McFarland | Murray Special |
| Wilmer Monahan | Brady Williams | Packard Special |
| Mike Hudoc | R. W. Patterson | Buick Special |
| N.P. Fetterman | Burton Bailey | Haynes Special |
| J.E. Conway | George J. Halley | Haynes Special |
| I.P. Fetterman | | Peerleass Special |
| H.L. Robinson | | Haynes Special |
| C.S. Jones | F.M. Carthyor | Stearns Knight |
| Alva Hughson | | Pathfinder |
| Barney Newgard | Emert N. Pala | Crawford |
| Arthur Klein | E.J. Longchamps | Crawford |
| F.M. Seanor | | Haynes Speciall |

The English Hughie Hughes was scheduled to give an exhibition in the 12 cylinder Sunbeam owned by a wealthy New York sportsman, Richard Adams. The car was accredited with 132mph on the Brooklands track. He had recently beat the speed king, Bob Burman in Corona, California with the Sunbeam. During that race Burman lost his life. He was driving what they afterward referred to as the "jinx car". Burman had built the car with a Puegeot motor and had reconstructed it making it several mph faster. Burman was known to be "the man who traveled the mile and kilometer faster than any man who ever lived." In Corona his car jumped a curb and the back wheel got caught in a steel cable from a telegraph pole trying to catch Hughes in the Sunbeam. The pole snapped like a toothpick as Burman had hit it at 106mph. At this 1916 Uniontown Speedway race, Burman's mechanic, Jack Cable was to drive the "jinx car", but was eliminated at the trials.

The Sunbeam had been disqualified from the Universal Trophy race because of its exceptional power. The piston displacement and motor were twice the size of the average race car. Officials also agreed the car could not take the strain from the 100 lap board race.

Elimination trials were held on Wednesday for the fastest professional drivers in the world. Trials had been scheduled to be held on Sunday, but this was stopped because the contract held with the Brownfield's (property owners), prohibited it. They were ready to compete for the $3,000.00 Universal Film Trophy. Carl Laemmle, President of the Universal Film Manufacturing

Company, donated the solid silver automobile racing trophy; the first offered this popular sport by any film company. This gesture, by such a powerful businessman, lent credibility to the track and racing around the world. Winners from Indianapolis, California, and New York tracks were revved up to smash speed records in the struggle to win the three feet tall work of art. The following prizes were offered:

### *The Universal Trophy Race, Class E, Non-Stock:*

First prize.......................................... $1,000.00
Second place.......................................... $700.00
Third place............................................$600.00
Fourth place..........................................$500.00
Fifth place............................................$100.00
The car leading on the 45th lap.............$100.00

### *W.D. Johnston Cup dealer's race, Class D, Non-Stock:*

First prize............................................$500.00
Second place..........................................$300.00
Third place............................................$200.00
Fourth place..........................................$100.00
Fifth place..............................................$50.00

## *Unique System of Timing and Recording this Race was Devised and Constructed by Local Men*

"The system of timing races on the U.S.A. Speedway differs vastly from the system in vogue at other speedways, and the racing drivers are loud in their praise of it. In this unique system are incorporated the salient points of all other timing systems and the improved unique ideas of some of the brightest minds of the electrical and mechanical world. A great amount of credit is due A.M. Crichton, of the Tri-State-Telephone company, for the successful completion of the timing system. The cars mechanically register their own time in crossing the starting line. The number of laps made are electrically registered simultaneously at the timing table, the field scoreboard and the pit, thereby eliminating the possibility of an error in registering the number of laps made. The U.S.A. scoreboard is the only speedway where the number of laps is electrically registered. This same is true with reference to the registering of laps in the pits. The time made by the leading car and the rate of speed at which the car is running is posted on the big scoreboard every eighth lap. This serves to keep the audience thoroughly posted on the progress of the race."

The Thanksgiving Day race was delayed because of rain until Monday December 2, but trials were held where Hughie Hughes clipped off several laps at 102mph. During these trials two serious accidents were caused by inexperienced drivers on the wooden track. They both disobeyed official's orders. One man locked his brakes up skidding into a crowd of officials and another broke a front axle. Five thousand people watched these trials at the admission fee of 25 cents each. Seats for the Universal race went for $1.00. Reserved seats ran $2.00 and $3.00 dollars.

# Driver's Biographies

Hughie Hughes was 30 and from England. He was known as one of the best race car driver's the world had thus far seen. In 1904 he drove a Detrich car in the Gordon Bennett race in France. He won the Savannah trophy in 1911. That same year he took third place in the grand prize race in an Ono. In 1914 he won the Tacoma Potlatch in a Maxwell. Since then he won several hill climbs with the Allen-Kingstons team. He established a record of 110mph at Indianapolis in Walter Christie's front drive car.

Arthur Klein was head of the Crawford team from Hagerstown, MD. He began racing in 1909 and made his way to Indianapolis by 1914. Reports show that it looked like he had a good chance to win that race, but he broke a valve stem about half way through. He came in 2nd soon after that in the Potlatch trophy race at Tacoma, WA and 3rd in the Mont marathon. He was winning the latter race, but acquired carburetor and tire troubles. He had raced around the country and found himself in Uniontown at the new speedway.

Barney Newgard was a member of the Crawford team. He had been around racing for some time. He was head mechanic of the winning Duisenberg team. He rode with Eddie O'Donnell until the accident in Kansas City. He then joined the Devlin team with Hughie Hughes driving.. When he joined the Crawford team he rode with Arthur Klein. This was his first driving race!

Frank Galvin began as a world class cyclist in both America and Europe. When he caught the car racing fever, he was in Europe driving a German Opel. He was the only American on a foreign team and soon ran a Buick "Bug" which caused quite a stir on dirt tracks. Galvin joined the famous Peugeot team which took him all over the U.S. and on to Indianapolis. He began driving a Sunbeam which won him cash prizes everywhere he went. In 1915 he finished 3rd in Cincinnati in a field of 32 starters. In New York's Harkness trophy race he came in 2nd setting world records for distance and averaging 106 mph. He was beat by Aitken, his teammate, by 9 seconds.

Ralph DePalma was born in Italy but lived in New York since early childhood. He was known for several years as the best all around race car driver yet seen. This judgement was made because of his courage, resourcefulness, and conservative driving. He was also known to be cool, steady, deliberate, and of heady character whether winning or losing. The man was always smiling and happy, with a lilt of cheerfulness in his voice. This is why he was followed by thousands of friends and fans.

DePalma was one of two drivers who had at that time

captured the Vanderbilt cup two consecutive times. He was unlucky in road races during his early career (1908-) but crowned "mile-track king" because of his success in track events. In the 1908 Grand Prix at Savannah he out-drove both American and European rivals only to brake a cylinder nearing the last lap. In 1908 he took 10 firsts and 3 seconds out of 16 starts; 1909 he won 34 out of 47 starts, came in second 8 times and third 1 time. He went on to win well over 100 track, speedway, and road races holding many records. In May 1914 he won the International 500-Mile Sweepstakes at Indianapolis, establishing a new record for the brick course.

Bert Watson was from New York and had been racing on dirt tracks and at all the Sheepshead Bay speedway races, placing in three.

M.F. McBride was Bert Watson's teammate and had the reputation of a nervy, cool courteous man about the tracks.

John DePalma was Ralph's brother. He was an up and coming driver and drove the Universal Film Trophy car from New York to Uniontown.

James Benedict hailed from New York and fully expected to take the trophy back there. He had attended the last Summit Mountain Hill Climb and had plenty of board track experience as well. He finished fifth in the 100-mile Harkness Gold Trophy Race at Sheepshead just a month before and brought his high powered car here in top condition.

Dave Lewis began driving dirt track races in 1902. Before that he was the amateur bicycle champion of California. In 1912 at Brighton Beach, New York, he won 20 out of 30 starts. He won several races at the Ascot track in California, and held the 100 mile beach race record at Old Orchard Beach, ME. He scored places in a number of races with the Stutz team and broke the world's 5 mile record in DeMoines; that same day winning the 50 mile race there. He also scored second in the Chicago Grand Prix, Tacoma Road Race, the Sioux City speedway races, and the 50 mile race in Omaha.

Otto Henning had raced for six years when entering the Uniontown opening race with an Ogren. This car showed a continued speed of 105mph on the two mile track in Chicago, going 115mph on the straights.

Louis Chevrolet came here from France in 1908 and started in the racing game as Hemery's mechanic. He was as famous as an automobile engineer as he was a race driver. When Hemery went back to France in 1909 Chevrolet started on a barnstorming trip in a Buick. That year he earned the distinction of being the first man to drive 70mph in a road race. He won the Long Island trophy contest then. He went about breaking records and driving in every

event he could get to. Chevrolet had invented the Frontenac car which was popular on the board track circuit. In 1918 his automobile firm was added to General Motors.

I.P. "Red" Fetterman came in 2nd in the 1915 Summit Mountain Hill Climb and was a locally famous driver hailing from Pittsburgh. He had piloted many dirt track races winning several and was here to race the entry of Hiland Automobile Company of Pittsburgh.

Wilmer "Monnie" Monahan drove the Packard Greyhound owned by the Standard Garage in Uniontown. He was known to be daring and fearless. This was his first race on a wooden track, but he had an enviable record on dirt.

Mike Hudoc of Uniontown piloted a Buick "Yellow Kid" owned by the Standard Garage. He was popular among local drivers and had a lot of dirt track experience.

Fred McCarthy worked for several years as the mechanic for Dario Resta, the world famous champion of the racing season. He was driving here for the Murray Motor Car Company and was known as a nervy capable opponent.

N.P. Fetterman, "Red's" brother, had been racing four years on dirt. He was one of the most popular Pittsburgh drivers.

# *How the Race was Run*

## *A Concise Account of How the Big Event was Managed*

SANCTION - The opening race was run under the supervision of the American Automobile Association, the governing body of the sport. F.H. Rosboro, official representative of the association was in supreme control, with Web Jay and A.M. Crichton assisting in the roles of starter and chairman of timing. Minor appointments were made only with the sanction of these officials.

JUDGES - The order of the finish in the event of a close race was decided by the board of judges, while cases of unfair driving were passed on by umpires stationed at regular intervals about the course.

ELIGIBILITY - Drivers must pass a physical examination before the race to assure physical fitness and capability. Cars were also inspected to be sure they did not exceed the 300 cubic inches allowed and to prove that vital parts such as front axles and steering connections had been placed at least two days before the races. On the morning of the race all entries have their brakes tested.

ELIMINATIONS - Of those entered only fifteen of the fastest cars could enter the professional race. Time trials were held to establish the top racers. They ran one lap each in the reverse order of entry.

START - The start was flying. All contestants were placed around the course by Pres. Charlie Johnson, accompanied by Carl Laemmle of Universal Films. When the starter's flag drops the first time around, the race has begun.

SCORING - The official scores were kept by hand because no devise had yet been invented that was as accurate as the old fashioned way. Ready information was displayed on a special scoring machine which had thirty odometers with push buttons attached. The device made it possible to arrive at lap and total standings instantaneously, for the benefit of the contestants.

ANNOUNCING - Announcers and scoreboards transmitted information as to the progress of the race to spectators. There were more than 250 men engaged in this work. Scoreboards were constantly checked through a telephone system centering in the judge's stand, while announcing data was supplied through the Speedway press bureau, which covered every inch of the ground with a network of telephone wires.

SIGNALS - Signal flags used by the starter and assistants were: Red, clear course; yellow, stop immediately; green, starting last lap; checkered, you are finished; white, stop for consultation; and blue, accident on course.

PRESS - The Press Stand accommodated 200 people, plus telegraph operators and the officials paddock, several hundred more. Information was furnished to these workers as quickly as possible and they relayed it through the myriad of trunk lines to all parts of the world. The day before the races more than 5,000 sport extras were published on the upcoming race. They had estimated that more than 25,000 publications would carry the opening day races the day after.

POLICE - Guards, detectives, and special officers were organized to keep spectators safe throughout the events.

HOSPITAL - A complete hospital was maintained on the speedway grounds with every facility to care for contestants.

## *Important Rules Governing the Race*

All automobile contests held in this country are conducted with the sanction and under the rules of the American Automobile Association. To a certain extent the same rules prevailing in road races govern contests on specially constructed courses, but the following may be cited as important speedway rules and will give a fair idea of what is expected of the contestants once the race is started:

The driver and mechanic of a car may be changed, if need be, during a race, but only at the end of a lap and upon application to the Referee. In case of disability or accident to the driver-but in no other case-the mechanic may replace him at any part of the course.

Should the mechanician leave his seat for any reason whatsoever at any time during the race, the driver must not continue until the mechanician is again seated in the car. In case of disability or accident to the mechanician which may necessitate his leaving the car, the driver may after stopping and investigating, proceed alone to the pits and make application to the referee for instructions.

All mechanical repairs and adjustments must be made exclusively by the crew of the car. At the repair pits each contestant entering one car is entitled to have five attendants, including the team manager. For each additional car entered by the same contestant, he is entitled to three pit attendants. In either case only two pit attendants shall be permitted to make replacement of gasoline, oil, and water and replacement or refreshment of tires, or crank the motor when contestant's car is at a standstill at the pits, but these attendants shall in no case make any mechanical repairs or adjustments to the car or assist in any manner in such repairs or adjustments.

Pit attendants are not allowed under any circumstances to pump air or oil into the car.

Spare parts, tools, etc. may be laid on the shelf or ledge in front of the pit, and pit attendants, while in the pit, but not otherwise, may hand same to the driver or mechanic. No car is permitted to leave its pit, until all tools, tires, etc., on the ground in front of the pit have been removed.

All renewals of fuel, oil, water and replenishments of damaged parts have to be made at the repair pits at the start and finish line, except in case of emergency. Where a car is disabled on the track and cannot exceed under its own power to the pits, the crew of the car may report to the referee, who, in his discretion may allow the crew to obtain necessary fuel and parts (except tires) as will enable the car to proceed under its own power. Such replenishments or replacements must be made by the crew unassisted.

Tires may be taken on at the pits, and, if necessary, at any section of the course, provided in the latter case that extra tires are carried on the car. Any competing car voluntarily leaving the course will be disqualified.

## *Event No. 2*

Any dealer whose residence is within 150 miles of Uniontown may enter in this event, one or more cars, of the same make he represents, providing the driver and mechanician also come within the residence qualification.

A dealer must be representative of a factory marketing pleasure cars and the cars entered must be of this manufacture. The car can be stripped and fitted with any gears, timed and tuned at the discretion of the dealer.

In addition to the general rules and conditions, note carefully the following approved special conditions which will apply to the Dealer's Race:

1st - All tires must be fastened on the rims with 13 lugs exclusive of valve lugs.

2nd - If more than 15 cars qualify, the following conditions will finally determine the starters:

a. The individual car of the make which is represented by the largest number of entries, making the best time in the official speed trials, will be awarded first starting position. Succeeding positions will be awarded in the same manner until the fastest cars of each make which is represented by more than one qualified entry shall have been placed.

b. The fastest cars representing makes of which only one car has qualified will then be given the next open starting positions in order.

c. If the methods outlined in the paragraphs do not fill fifteen positions, the starters in the remaining positions will be determined by a special five-lap race, open only to the remaining cars which have qualified in the official speed trials, but have been eliminated by the above conditions, to be held on the last day of the qualifying trials (November 29th), and the order of finish of the necessary number of cars in this event will govern, except that under no conditions may more than three cars of any one make start.

***This was the headline the day before the races:***

## *Drivers Hope to Smash Records on Speedway Tomorrow*

***This was the headline the evening after the races:***

# *Hughes And Weigle Dead; Galvin To Die*

### *Galvin's Premier Hits Press Stand; Kills Two At Once; Injures Several; Chevrolet Wins 20,000 See Races*

On a bright and sunny December 2, 1916, the Uniontown Speedway opened its gates. It was a proud day for the county seat and all of racing. The new board track was said to be of superior construction compared to those built in prior years. Universal Film stars and businessmen caught the eyes of the thousands of spectators when they weren't watching the track. The town and mountains were filled to capacity. Hotels, restaurants, and shops saw their biggest intakes in the history of the area. From starlets to farmers, they were all there. Those who could not get into the arena watched from the hoods of cars and the backs of their horses from surrounding knobs. It was estimated that another 10,000 watched from outside the fences.

Imagine the excitement! Famous drivers from all over the world revved up their engines, and life was good for Fayette Countians. They were in the national and international spotlight. The money and prestige were rolling in. At 9am a Salute was held. At 9:30 , 10:30, and 11:30 a "Bomb" with 25 tickets for the May 1917 Grand Opening Race was put off. At noon Hughie Hughes held a 1 mile exhibition in a 12 cylinder Sunbeam. After another Salute and Figured shell, Hughes ran a five mile run to set a record. 1pm saw the brake test. At 1:30 a Salute was held. Cars were put in position and drivers and mechanics lined up for a photo, parade and introduction of drivers. At 1:50 a Salute and ten minute signal was given. 2pm -the American flag with a U.S.A. pennant and ticket bomb. This started the 100-lap race.

Hughie Hughes was to run a 10 mile exhibition later, but on the 64th lap he ran his Hoskins high on the lower turn to pass Frank Galvin and got into a pocket making it necessary to swerve sharply to the left in order to avoid hitting Galvin. He coasted over the turn and into the guardrail driving through the fences at least 100 yards into the field. George Titlow ran out to escort the driver from his car. As they walked over to the press stand, Hughes reached out to shake his car owner's hand (J.C. Hoskins). Glavin's Premier unaccountably turned directly toward the press stand. Hughes was crushed when Galvin, who Hughes had just sacrificed the race for, hit him head on, smashing the famous driver to his death. The Premier then plowed into the press box where 100 people watched in terror. The machine overturned killing the riding mechanic Gaston Weigle. Galvin died two days later, never knowing what happened. The other drivers agreed that the knowledge of how the accident happened would have killed him, had he survived. F.W. Kelly was hurled head first into the press stand and died as did an unknown man, bringing the death toll to five for the day. Mont W. McCormick suffered a broken leg and many who were injured were taken to the Uniontown Hospital. The track was closed to the public as the race went on. The drivers did not know how serious the accident was until the end of the race.

Louis Chevrolet won the trophy cup with a time of 1 hour 14 minutes, 12 and 2/5 seconds. Dave Lewis took 2nd, Ralph DePalma 3rd, and Barney Newgard tied Milt McBride for the 4rth and 5th spots. 105mph was the top speed set by Ralph DePalma. The dealer's race was wrought with excitement, too. The Haynes car number 9 driven by J. Conway, caught fire just 100 yards from the grand stand. The track also caught fire but was saved. The car was a total loss. I.P. Fetterman drove the last 18 miles of this race with a wooden splinter in his eye, winning with an average speed of 80mph. Fred McCarthy came in 2nd, and H.L. Robinson was 3rd.

The entire race was filmed by Universal Studios. It is said that track officials and cameramen came to blows while camermen were filming the blood bath that occurred when Galvin hit the press box. The film of the entire opening day's action was shown for four days at Uniontown theatres.

As the press box collapsed, Alex W. Frerich, a local reporter who was buried under the debris, found himself next to the telephone. He phoned Mary Kate O'Bryon at the Evening Standard and relayed the amazing story as it occurred. This race made headlines all over the world and still goes down in history as one of the most tragic races of all time.

# *Yesteryear At The Uniontown Speedway 1917*

## *May 10, 1917 Grand Opening Race*

The grand stand was finished and the track in fine form as Uniontown prepared for the Grand Opening Race of their new speedway board track. It was scheduled for May 10 and the following column appeared in the Uniontown Morning Herald May 4:

## *Greatest Set of Drivers and Cars in Country Here for Races*

By Barney Oldfield

"I am glad to get to Uniontown. For many years I have heard of the big little city so full of sportsmanship, but having no track here until recently. I have not raced here during my 17 years at the wheel of racing cars.

I have been here only six hours but in that short space of time I have been shown such evidence of fellowship that I feel quite at home and know I shall be sorry when the time comes to leave.

For constructing such a magnificent racing plant as the Uniontown Speedway Association has built, you deserve all the credit in the world and I know that the racing fraternity appreciates what has been done for the motor sport here. Every one of the boys feels obligated to put forth his best effort to give the crowd a run for its money. You have a greater set of cars and drivers here than any speedway can boast of this year. Half of them are here like myself just to show Charlie Johnson and the Uniontown people that good sportsmanship must be rewarded.

I never pick myself to win a race, consequently I will have to talk about the chances of the others. I believe the race lies between DePalma, Chevrolet, and Eddie Hearne if the dope counts for much. DePalma's new Packard is lightening fast and if it goes through without trouble he ought to cop the money. Chevrolet knows the track and his car and it has a world of speed. Hearne has a fast car and is a great driver. He has always dealt out surprises in the big races and I am never surprised at what he pulls at the finish of a speed battle. But no matter who is evolved winner they can all say after he gets the checkered flag, "Well, he was certainly going some."

At this time Barney was a famous driver and all-around character, referred to as "the daddy of them all" in the grand opening race program.. He was rarely seen without a cigar and had been wowing race fans for two decades when he came to Uniontown. He had laid low for a few years but came to Indianapolis in 1916 surprising thousands when he became the first American driver to finish in the record breaking grind. He then went on to win the Los Angeles to Phoenix 671 mile Desert race scoring several non-stop records. Oldfield was given his start as a driver when Henry Ford built a race car and hired him to drive. Ford was not making much profit selling cars and wished to bring in prize money. Oldfield drove the #999 to win the money several times.

Tryouts for the big race were held May 3. This day Louis Chevrolet set a new record of 99mph on the oval track, only to outdo himself at 100mph during qualifying trials May 7. Drivers were required to average a speed of 85mph in order to compete in the races.

During the trials, pilot "Dutch" DeLloyd Thompson of the New York National Guard, was hired to entertain crowds with his death defying antics. There was a "scenic fort" built in the speedway's infield. Numerous "bombs" were fired from the fort into the sky at the military "tractor". As Thompson turned loop the loop he fired one shell that failed to explode as a spark head flew off, propelling itself through the covering of the plane's engine. This made it necessary for the daring pilot to cut the engine and volplane from 3,000 feet above the earth. He did this gracefully, showing his nerve and "cool" as a top notch pilot. Charlie Johnson asked "Dutch" if he could entertain at the grand opening race the next May, and he said that he would be proud to do it.

The list of entries for the Universal Trophy were as follows:

Event No. 1 Class E, Non-Stock,
300 Cubic Inches Piston Replacement, or under,
100 laps, 112 1/2 miles.

| Number | Car | Driver and Mechanician |
|---|---|---|
| 1 | Frontenac Special | Louis Chevrolet,Charles Kirkpatrick |
| 2 | Mercedes " | Louis Fountain,H.P. Miller |
| 3 | Frontenac " | Joe Boyer, Jr.Roscoe Searles |
| 4 | Packard " | Ralph DePalma, James Steaks |
| 5 | Duesenberg " | Eddie Hearne,Lewis Lecoca |
| 7 | Newman " | Billy Taylor,M.L. Spence |
| 9 | Hudson " | Ralph Mulford,Ernest Olsen |
| 12 | Hoskins " | Dave LewisRussell Burns |
| 14 | Hudson " | Ira Vail,Barney Newgard |
| 15 | Pugh " | J.A. Meyer,G. Frazier |
| 17 | Crawford " | H.E. McCord |
| 21 | Olsen " | Milt McBride,L.C. Raynor |
| 24 | Johnson " | Art Klein,Wiler Monahan |
| 27 | Delage " | Barney Oldfield,Waldo Stein |
| 42 | Erbes " | Andy Burt,M.J. Hudoc |

Event No. 2, Class E--
Special Invitation Dealer's Race.
Non-Stock without regard to piston displacement limitation.
100 laps, 112 1/2 miles.

List of entries Dealer's Race:

| **Number** | **Car** | **Driver - Mechanician** |
|---|---|---|
| 28 | Murray " | C.W. McFarland,Charles Seitz |
| 31 | Peerless " | I.P. Fetterman,P.W. Robinson |
| 32 | Buick " | M. Hudoc,D.W. Hickey |
| 33 | Packard " | W. Monahan,C.M. Williams |
| 34 | Haynes " | H.L. Robinson,E.F. Marsh |
| 35 | Oakland " | J.P. Snyder |
| 37 | Haynes " | N.P. Fetterman |
| 41 | Haynes " | F. McCarthy,R.M. Shoff |
| 22 | Murray " | H.E. Wynn,L.E. James |

Program Cover for the Grand Opening Race, May 10, 1917

The afternoon before the races Ray Hazen, mechanic for Driver C.M. Ewan of Kentucky, was injured when their Crawford shot up the incline of the speedway course during qualifications, broke through the top guard rail and teetered on the top of the steep track's edge. It then spun like a top down the track crashing into the lower guard rail. Hazen, of Kansas City, was thrown out onto his head when they hit the upper rail. He rolled down the track just next to the wild car. He sustained a concussion and many minor injuries. They were disqualified because of the car's extensive damage.

Mr. Ricker (referee) addressed all the drivers the night before the races in the lodge room of the First National Bank Building and told them what was expected of them and that the rules would be strictly enforced. The morning of the races the weather man promised fair skies and the Uniontown Speedway Association announced, "Nothing but a downpour of rain this afternoon can cause a postponement of the grand opening classic of the Uniontown speedway."

## *World's Greatest Drivers Compete For Fine Trophy*

The following are biographies of some of the drivers. Oldfield, DePalma, Chevrolet, Klein, etc., have been discussed earlier:

J.A. Meyer had driven his Pugh at Sheepshead Bay three times, taking 3rd in a special 5-mile race. He was expected by the "wise ones" to finish strong as he was an enthusiastic driver, a glutton for work, and his good nature endeared him to fans.

Milton F. McBride drove an Olsen Special in last year's race with considerable credit and was touted as a real contender.

"Smiling" Ralph Mulford was stock champion and one-time winner of the Vanderbilt Cup. He was known to wear white linen during the races, along with his smile.

Eddie Hearne was a well known driver who participated with credit in many of the professional events for years. In 1910 he won the Fox River Cup Race at Elgin in his Mercedes and finished eighth in the Vanderbilt Cup Race. He then went on to win the Fernbank Road Race in Cincinnati and a variety of dirt track events. His fans and friends considered him a strong contender.

Ira Vail was merely in his second season of racing, but had a reputation as he won almost every dirt track race he ever entered. He was a wealthy Brooklyn

fellow who had raced motorcycles at Brighton Beach Motor dome and raced in the 100 mile contest at the Providence Speedway just months before.

Walter W. Longstreth 26, was from Rosemont, PA. He was known in Pennsylvania, New Jersey, and New York to be certain to finish "in the money".

Louis Fountain was Ralph DePalma's mechanic for many years. Here he gained invaluable experience as an up and coming driver. This was his third big race and he was respected throughout the racing circuit.

W.E. Taylor, hailing from the west coast, had won in the top three or five in a variety of national races, both dirt and road.

## *Schedule of Events*

8AM - Two late entrants, Wynn and Robinson will qualify for Dealer's race.
8:15 - noon Practice runs by the big drivers at the discretion of Referee Ricker
Noon - Course closed.
1 o'clock - Dealer's Race 112 miles
2:50 - Aeroplane flight by DeLloyd Thompson
3 o'clock - Universal Trophy race

At 6PM the special trains which brought thousands of fans from every small town imaginable between Uniontown and Pittsburgh and into West Virginia, will run their return trips.

Folks were advised of two entrances to the park. Grand stand and box ticket holders could park free by the grand stand after taking the Country Club Road route. All others were to use the main entrance on the National Pike. It cost $1.00 for adults. Children under 12 got in free, and the day's program could be had for a mere 15 cents.

The new Technical Committee Chairman this year was Chester Ricker from Indianapolis. John Donahue assisted Rosboro as Referee, Zed Springer assisted Neil Whalen as Starter, Searight Marshall was Director of Scoring, William Pickens of Chicago, was Manager of Publicity, Jess Johnson served as scoreboard manager, and all other officials were the same as the first race the year before.

Members of the Keystone provided Police protection with Chief Williams and the Hook and Ladder, and Union Hose companies under the direction of Robert Seese, assisted by Edwin Howard.

Keystone members: Ray Keener, captain; George Mathews, Earl Deane, C.M. Wiley, C.C. Scott, George Ashman, Mason McLaughlin, and Arthur Bradley.

Chief Williams - George Little, captain; Ray Fields, J.R. Benson, Albert Griffith, Bowman Roth, Lloyd Bixler, William Thompson, and Charles Doran.

Union Hose - F.B. Wood, captain; M. Raffle, L. Harford, J. Onttko, S. Hill, George Cook, F. Swartz, and U.G. Markley.

The D. M. Bierer Rifle Club Band sang the Star Spangled Banner and My Country Tis of Thee just before gun shot at the starting line.

Barney Oldfield's Golden Submarine is pictured left front of this picture. Billy Taylor's car #5 is shown to the right. He was the Universal Trophy Race winner this day.

May 10, 1917 Grand Opening Universal Trophy Auto Derby. In the center of the photograph is Barney Oldfield standing sideways with neck scarf. Louis and Gaston Chevrolet are the third and fourth men in the back row to Oldfield's right. They are sporting thick mustaches. Smiling Ralph Mulford is waving and grinning in white coveralls to the left of the group in white. Billy Taylor's car #5 is shown. He was the Universal Trophy race winner this day. Louis Chevrolet's #8 is on the right.

Grandstands were filled to capacity for the great grand opening race.

Carl Laemmle, President of the Universal Film Manufacturing Company, donor of the famous $3,000 solid silver automobile speed trophy, the first incentive offered this famous and popular sport by any film industry, was hailed by the sporting world as one of the greatest assets in the promotion of clean contests.

Mr. Laemmle, by his generous act gave added impetus to a sport of which the world will never tire, and in May, the second contest for the possession of this handsome coveted trophy will take place on the Uniontown Speedway. Already all the prominent drivers of America have signified their intention to compete, and records will be smashed in the struggle for it.

Mr. Laemmle has always been a patron of out door sports, and when, while busily engaged as the head of the greatest film manufacturing company in the world, he took time and trouble to attend to the details of arranging for the Universal Film Trophy, he proved his real sportmanship in a fashion rarely equalled in sports.

The Universal Film Trophy was made by hand of solid silver and is one of the finest ever made by Black, Starr and Frost. It stands thiry-six inches high and measures fifty-two inches around the base. Three months were taken in the making of the trophy, and it stands as an unequalled example of the silversmith's art.

Mr.. Laemmle's donation to the speed game injected a new life into it, and the forthcoming contest will be the great sporting event of the year.

THE UNIVERSAL FILM TROPHY

Uniontown Speedway Association announces the engagement of

# DE LLOYD THOMPSON

## World's Premier Aviator

in a Thrilling Exhibition of Fancy Flying
Looping the Loop,
and Flying Upside Down

MAY 10th, 1917

Mr. Thompson will conduct a school for aviators volunteering for the aviation corps

DeLloyd Thompson and Lieut. George Robertson of N. Y. National Guard in Thompson's Military Tractor fitted with rapid-fire gun

For information about aviation school or exhibition flying engagements, address Wm. H. Pickens, Westminster Building, Chicago

# *Universal Trophy To "Dark Horse" In A No-stop Run*

## *Oldfield, DePalma, and Hudson Team Frequently Forced to Pits and Suffer Irretrievable Delays*

### *How The Big Race Was Run*

Billy Taylor of Los Angeles, California took the Universal Cup from Louis Chevrolet when engine trouble caused the Frenchman to fall behind a full two laps. Although he came back on the track at ferocious speed, he could not make up the boards that had been lost. Taylor was virtually unknown in the east, but because the famous speed kings had their problems, Taylor won the Universal Trophy and could keep it permanently if he won it two more consecutive times. Taylor drove a beautiful Stutz car owned by oil man Fred Newman, of Oklahoma. He drove the entire 112 miles without a stop on an average of 89.25 mph, completing the course in 1 hour, 15 minutes, and 38 seconds. The Hudson team of Ira Vail and Ralph Mulford had trouble not long after the race began, Mulford's car getting "out of whack " and Vail had to replace tires and work on the engine. Chevrolet got a lap ahead of DePalma and Vail, keeping the lead for 80 laps.

Billy Taylor wowed the crowd in his red racer when he shortened the gap between himself and the famous Louis Chevrolet. Eddie Hearne closed in on Taylor in the last quarter and for 15 to 20 laps there was a great race with Chevrolet holding a 1 lap lead. That is when Chevrolet hit the pits for engine repairs.

Taylor had run many west coast races over the last 7-8 years, but this was the first race he had ever won. Newman had hired him just three months before this race and this was the first time he had raced the new Stutz car. After the races Newman said he would provide Taylor with the best in race cars because he had a barrel full of money to spend and Taylor was the best.

When Taylor crossed the tape on his 100th lap, Oldfield was on his 89th, DePalma on his 79th, Vail his 71st, and Mulford on his 90th lap respectively. The other drivers completed their laps and it was an entire 10 minutes before the last car was given the checkered flag.

### *The Race Results*

Universal Trophy

1 Billy Taylor
2 Joe Boyer
3 Eddie Hearnes
4 Louis Chevrolet
5 Dave Lewis
6 Art Klein
7 Jimmy Myer
8 Ralph Mulford
9 Barney Oldfield
10 Milt McBride
11 Ralph DePalma

Dealer's Race

1 I.P. "Red" Fetterman
2 Fred McCarthy
3 H.E. Wynn
4 H.L. Robinson
5 M.J. Hudoc

In the first 50 miles of the dealer's race Wilmer Monahan in Charlie Johnson's Packard and Charles McFarland in his Murray gave the fans some thrills. Monahan then left the race during the 60th lap and McFarland was ruled off the course for "hogging" the upper guard rail. After Monahan wore his car out, Fetterman began pushing his racer harder and took over the race from the 80th lap on. He won by half a lap and ran out of gas just after he crossed the tape. McCarthy claimed that Fetterman had only made 99 laps but was overruled by the referee and told he could file a complaint if he wished.

In the Morning Herald the day after the race Uniontown Speedway President Charlie Johnson wrote: "I am very glad that such a huge crowd witnessed the running of Thursday's Speedway events for they saw the realization of the hopes and plans of the officials of the Speedway Association. The greatest lot of famous motor drivers piloting the mightiest lot of racing cars ever seen on a speedway battled for the supreme speed honors. And there were no accidents to mar the sport, proving that the track is absolutely safe after it was completed and that the unfortunate accident last December was not the fault of the course. When fifteen such cars and drivers as started Thursday can go through such a grueling contest without the semblance of an accident there is not much more to be said in praise of the most spectacular and fastest "less than two miles" speedway in the world.

"The name Uniontown has been printed thousands of times and will be printed many thousand more times in papers all over the country as a result of the speedway auto races. Such publicity can not be bought. The people here need never fear that they can mention the name of their city while traveling and fail to hear the other fellow remark about this being the city "that has the speedway.

"The city was full of people Wednesday night, Thursday, last night and will be crowded for a couple more days. That's the material benefit the city derives from the speedway.

"The ticket sellers and our auditors were busy all last night and will be busy a part of today counting the money. There was a lot of it, certainly not less than $50,000.00 and the race will show a handsome profit. From an investment alone, the speedway will pay handsome returns to the stockholders."

Dutch Thompson put on a spectacular show in his biplane. He hails from Washington County and many of his fans were there to cheer him on as he did six somersaults at an altitude of 3,000 feet. There were 40,000 people at the speedway this day when they announced that Thompson would hold a government aviation school in Uniontown.

The Uniontown Speedway Association immediately planned a Dealer's Race for the fourth of July. The afternoon before the holiday, during trials, Car #45 of the Mercer team swerved up the track on the south west turn. It then crashed into the guard rail at 86mph, turned around twice and came to a stop at the inner rail. Driver Boettcher stayed in his seat, but mechancian Desautel was thrown out of the car onto his head as it slid down the steep embankment. Desautel scraped his arm but was not seriously injured. The men assured fans that the car looked worse than it was and that they would be in the race the next day. A twisted rear end and bent frame were the problems they had to solve overnight.

Dave Lewis, sole survivor of the Trinity Lewis-Galvin-Hughes who were among the star attractions in December's fatal opening race, quietly drove the Hoskins onto the track. Hughie

Hughes was on his way to driving the scarlet racer to fame when his life was cut short. Lewis meant to make Hughes proud and did when he entered the fastest qualifying time to date, 99 8/10mph. Even though he had set a record, Lewis knew he could do better and asked permission to run an exhibition lap to break the lap record held by Louis Chevrolet. He beat the Frenchman's record of 100mph by a fraction -100 1/4mph- and the crown was passed to the veteran driver. The "dope" around local hotels and garages had bets on Eddie Hearne to win, with Ralph Mulford, and Louis Chevrolet second and third.

The race for July 4th was postponed because weather observer Pennywit "pulled a bone" in his forecast, predicting rain showers. Twenty thousand fans and speedway officials moaned and groaned as the sun shone beautifully over Hopwood throughout the day.

I am sure the facts that the Fayette County Court requested that "no liquors be sold" on the Fourth of July in hotel bars and fireworks sales had been halted, called for the most quiet Independence Day in the history of the county seat. According to the papers, "mountain parties and other aversions will hold sway."

Joe Boyer won the three heat professional race, beating out Cooper and Vail. Boyer was driving Chevrolet's Frontenac. It was in the last heat that the four drivers really showed who the race was between. Vail's Hudson blew a tire at the beginning of the race. This was changed in 12 seconds while Cooper gained 1 1/2 laps on the Hudson. Vail pushed his racer to 106mph and caught Cooper on the 6th lap. They stayed together for 10 more laps, almost catching Boyer because his right rear tire was almost burned completely off. He had to slow down, especially on the curves, and limped across the finish line a full 1/4 mile ahead of his opponents. Vail failed to catch up after losing ground when changing that tire and Cooper lagged behind because he believed the other cars were inferior and would not stand the pressure. Wrong. Boyer won $1,500.00 in the champion event.

I.P. Fetterman won the dealer's race in his Peerless setting a record average speed of 92mph. This record was taken from Chevrolet. Wilber Monahan blew a tire and spun around three times on the southwest bank, but luckily no real accident occurred. Fetterman won $1,250.00 in the dealer's and Australian Pursuit races. Denny Hickey did well in this race, but could not keep up with Fetterman's Peerless.

Dutch Thompson wowed the crowds once more with his flying antics and the speedway association went on to plan a fall classic race as they were on a roll.

# *Henderson And Milton Put Up Good Race*
# *Chevrolet And Mechanician Hurt*

The 150 lap Autumn Classic held October 28 had to be postponed twice because of bad weather. This lessened the crowd by thousands, but drivers put on a show with Duesenburgs leading the way. Eddie Hearne crossed the finish line with his teammate Tommy Milton just behind him. Denny Hickey of Dawson, Pennsylvania came in 3rd in his Hudson, an up and coming driver everyone agreed. Milton had been leading the way but blew a tire in the 145th lap and had to drive like a demon to catch Hearne.

The starting line up was as follows:

Eddie Hearne, #45 Duesenberg
Tommy Milton, #7 Duesenberg
Dennis W. Hickey, #59 Hudson
Jimmy Meyers, #48 Pugh
Ora F. Haibe, #81 Pale
Ira Vail, #14 Hudson
Fred McCarthy, #41 Hudson
Dave Lewis, #12 Hoskins
Jack Conway, #56 Hudson
Ralph Mulford, #9 Frontenac
Pete Henderson, #8 Duesenberg
Gaston Chevrolet, #44 Frontenac
Barney Newgard, #29 Johnson
Gil Anderson, #55 Miller
Andy Burt, #42 Erbes

The initial laps were turned at an average speed of 93 1/3mph. Haibe was already out of the race from motor trouble in the 4th lap. Ira Vail took a long lead on the 11th and burnt up the track trying to keep it. On the 15th lap Vail was followed by Hearne, Hickey, and Henderson with speed mounting to an average of 95 3/5mph. Newgard went out in the 16th when a connecting rod broke on the Johnson Special. Vail was still leading in the 20th lap, completing 3 laps consecutively at over 100mph. Lewis' flat tire in the 22nd was changed in 10 seconds, Haibe went back to the pits, and Anderson also had motor trouble. After 25 laps the race was between Vail, Milton, Mulford, Hearne, Henderson, Hickey, and G. Chevrolet in that order. The speed was 96 4/5mph and this was faster than any previous race. Chevrolet skidded into the pits during the 34th lap to change a tire, which he did in 15 seconds, but not before he spun the Frontenac around twice. Vail pulled into the pits in the 37th lap and got out of the car. He had taken ill with stomach problems and was quickly replaced by driver Eddie Devoe who failed to recoup the lead. Mulford was leading in the 40th and Chevrolet gave his overheated motor a shot of water in the 46th. Milton took the lead in the next lap when Mulford took to the pits with engine trouble that took him out of the race. Hickey was at this point driving a powerfully heady race. At the 50th Milton, Henderson, Hearne, and Hickey were giving the crowds a show when Hickey went into the death curve in a pocket. He was surrounded by five racers when he blew a tire. The papers touted his driving as "an exhibition of the most skillful driving ever seen at this speedway" because he righted the vehicle, worked it down to the pole, and drew up to the pits amid thunderous applause. Hickey had just escaped death. He had yet another flat tire three laps later and Milton had the lead. The pace was now 93 3/5mph with Henderson and Hearne following the Duesenberg in their Duesenbergs. Milton blew a tire in the 72nd, spinning three times and making a quick change. When he went back in Henderson led the way. At lap 100 the three Duesenbergs were four full laps ahead of the other cars. Nine cars out of the 15 starters remained. Henderson blew a tire on death curve on the 122th lap. The car skidded, spun around several times, and came to a crashing halt against the inside guard rail. This demolished the car, but no injuries occurred.

On lap 135 Gaston Chevrolet hit the fence along the back stretch of the track at 100mph. Chevrolet and his mechanic Barbonini, were thrown out of the Frontenac. They had many injuries, but none were thought to be life threatening. Fans raced to the scene as the big scoreboard blocked the view of the wreck from most spectators. Milton blew a tire in the 145th lap and Hearne went on to cross the finish line first.

There were Championship Heats run this day, also, with Fred McCarthy driving the Connellsville Hudson to take home the trophy in #59 for Mr.. Stickel.

Fall classic 1917. On the left side of the photo is Augustus Stickel's Hudson #59. The Connellsville Hudson dealer stands fifth from the left. Barney Oldfield is to his right with cigar. Red Fetterman is between the men.

September 3, 1917 Labor Day Sweepstakes. The Miller team from left to right are A.A. Caldwell and Andy Burt with their mechanics by their sides. Joe Boyer is second to the left of Caldwell. Eddie Hearne is second to the right of Burt. On Hearne's right is Dawson driver, Denny Hickey.

The crowd is entertained by the band shown in the center of this photo, awaiting the big race.

Thousands of race fans fill the grandstands for the third big race in the history of the Uniontown Speedway.

I believe this is Fred McCarthy, in his Hudson #41. McCarthy won the trophy in this 1917 Fall Classic in the #59 Hudson. The driver also resembles Andy Burt. Can anyone clarify this?

Gus Stickel of Mount Pleasant poses proudly with a family heirloom earned by his grandfather's Hudson #59 at the Uniontown Speedway. The front of the trophy reads: Uniontown Speedway Challenge Trophy for Track Champions -1917- Between I.P. Fetterman, holder of the Track Record and the unknown winners of the 150 lap Autumn Classic Saturday October 20th 1917. The back says: Winner F. McCarthy - Car Hudson 59 Distance 50 laps 56 1/4 miles - Time 36 min. 12-60 sec. M.P.H. 93.26 in competition with Dave Lewis - Hoskins Special I.P. Fetterman - Peerless Special.

Uniontown Speedway Challenge Trophy October 1917, right.

# *Yesteryear At The Uniontown Speedway 1918*

Since President Wilson declared war in 1917 "to make the world safe for Democracy", many of the young racers and racing managers had been called into service. Billy Taylor who had won the second annual Universal Cup that past year, was shot down over France and crashed to his death. Others who had entered the service at that time were Art Klein, Eddie Rickenbacher, Charlie Ewan, and Ora Haibe. Neil Whalen had been made captain in charge of a tank regimen.

## *Big Crowd Is At Speedway Races Today*

Papers thrilled that there were hundreds more fans at the board track for the May 1918 season opener Liberty Sweepstakes than ever before. Fair weather blessed Hopwood as the Uniontown Military Band and singer Helen Rush entertained during the day's preliminary warm-ups. A patriotic war address was given by Reverand E.A. Hodil. The Universal Race had twelve drivers and consisted of four heats of 24 miles/27 laps. The winner of each heat competed in the final heat. Five thousand dollars in gold was distributed to the winners, the largest pot being $1,500.00 in the final heat. A Special Three Heat Match was run for the World's Track Championship where they ran 3 heats of 10 laps/11 1/4 miles each. Barney Oldfield and Louis Chevrolet competed in this with Oldfield taking his Golden Sub over the finish line two car lengths ahead of the popular Frenchman, for a pot of gold worth $5,000.00.

The May 16, 1918 Liberty Sweepstakes Universal Race entrants were:

| Driver | Entrant | Car |
|---|---|---|
| Eddie Hearne | L. Chevrolet | Frontenac Special |
| L. Chevrolet | L. Chevrolet | Frontenac " |
| | Omar Toft | Duesenberg |
| I.P. "Red" Fetterman | F.D. Saupp | Peerless |
| Omar Toft | Omar Toft | Miller |
| George B. Gardner | George B. Gardner | Hudson |
| Thomas Milton | A.S. Deusenberg | Duesenberg |
| Fred McCarthy | Fred McCarthy | Hudson |
| R.K. Mulford | R.K. Mulford | Frontenac |
| R.M. Shoff | Lawrence Motor Company | Lawrence |
| Denny Hickey | Fred McCarthey | Duesenberg |
| Ira Vail | Ira Vail | Hudson |
| Barney Oldfield | Barney Oldfield | Oldfield's Golden Sub |
| Louis LeCocq | Louis LeCocq | Roamer |

## *R. Mulford Takes Third Trophy Leg*

The final heat was between Mulford, Milton, L. Chevrolet, and Eddie Hearne. Milton had a safe lead in the first heat. Oldfield made headway in the second start, but was bowled over by Mulford. Eddie Hearne beat Fred McCarthy in the third spring after a heady match. Chevrolet took the fourth heat, but Ira Vail and I.P. Fetterman were disqualified after accidents which hurt their automobiles more than their persons. Dutch Thompson was in the grand stand, but did not have the government's permission to take to the air, so there was no aerial show that day. Even though the war was on, the gate receipts for this race were $40,000.00.

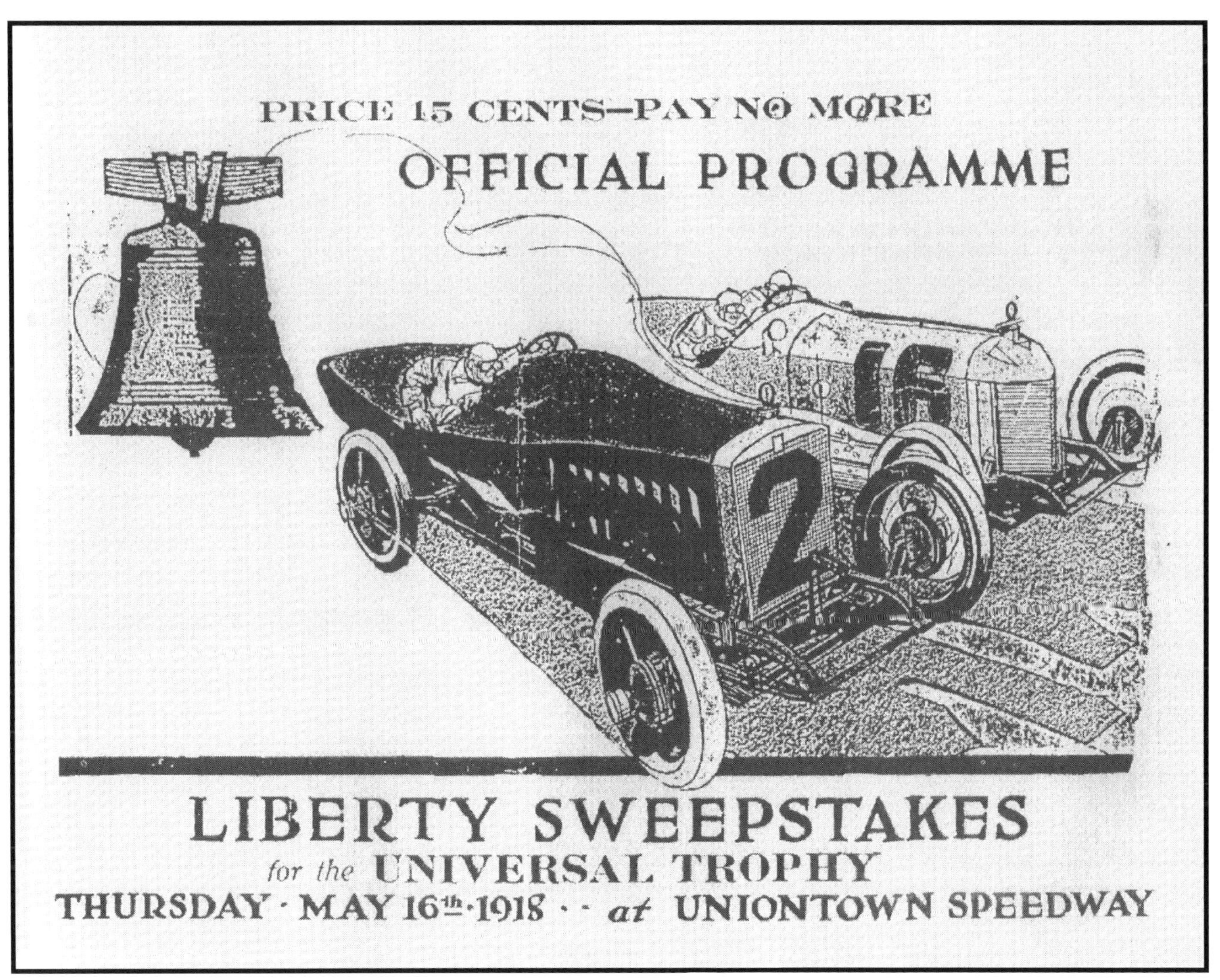

May 16, 1918 Liberty Sweepstakes Universal Trophy Race. To the left is Smiling Ralph Mulford in knickers, white shirt, and bow tie. The next man is unknown, then comes Louis Chevrolet, next two unknown, Augustus Stickel in suit, next five unknown, Denny Hickey, unknown, Barney Oldfield, and Tommy Milton. On the far right, second from right, is J.A. Meyer in white with crossed arms.

May 16, 1918 – Liberty Sweepstakes Universal Trophy Race – Sixth from left is "Smiling" Ralph Mulford, dressed in knickers, white shirt and bow tie. Second man to his right is Louis Chevrolet, next two unknown, Augustus Stickel in suit, Red Fetterman and Neil Whalen.

The following headline appeared in the Morning Herald July 16, 1918:

## *Milton Smashes Track Record At 107 Miles An Hr.*

Tommy Milton, driver for the Duesenberg team, used his powerful 12 cylinder Roamer to turn the fastest lap ever run on the Uniontown Speedway in the qualifying trials the day before the big races. This proved the speedway association's claim that the track had the ability to produce speeds up to 106mph. Just after he caught his breath in the pits, Milton told reporters, "The boys will have to beat the Roamer and your Uncle Tom Thursday to get the money. Both myself and my car are ready for the best race of the season."

Barney Oldfield had been "big brother" to Milton for years on the racing circuit and had this retort for his protégé, "You know what the Golden Sub did to Chevrolet on the 16th. She is faster than ever today and if you get the checkers before I do you'll know that you have been through one real automobile race. It won't be a joy ride, boy." Oldfield began his racing career when Henry Ford was having trouble making a profit selling automobiles and decided to build a race car to raise prize money. Oldfield was hired as the driver for Ford's #999 and won several races for him.

On July 17, Charlie Johnson met with the United States Fuel Administration and agreed to hold the races at 3pm to allow coal production a full day's work as the war was on. The Independence Day Auto Derby was held July 18, 1918. Milton, Chevrolet, Mulford, and Hickey were slated as top contenders for the money.

## *Chevrolet Is Invincible On Local Saucer*

For the second time, Louis Chevrolet took first place on the Uniontown Speedway Boardtrack. At the beginning of the 100 lap grind, I.P. Fetterman's green Peerless caught fire and was damaged beyond repair, disqualifying a fine contender. Just minutes later, George Gardner failed to notice the red "no start" flag and slammed into a group of cars that were making their preliminary lap to the flying start line. They were moving along at about 45mph when Gardner shot up at them going 80mph. Omar Toft, Dutch Thompson, Tom Milton, and Fred McCarthy had their race cars twisted about; Gradner's turning quickly over. Gardner and McCarthy were put out of the race, but no one was injured. During the first ten laps old timer Barney Oldfield led Chevrolet on his hardest chase of the entire race. After ten laps Oldfield's tires gave up which put him out long enough to totally lose first place for the day. Twice Chevrolet stopped for tire changes losing his leads to Mulford and then Toft. Hearne had a sure second place in the 99th lap when he blew a tire 200 yards from the grandstand, stomped his brakes so he could stop at the pits and turned the car around. This lost his 2nd place to Toft; Hearne taking 3rd, Mulford 4th, Milton, 5th, and Oldfield 6th.

Other races held that day were:

The International Match Race where Oldfield beat Arthur Duray.

Chevrolet beat Milton in a 5 lap scoot and Hearne beat Mulford in another 5 lapper.

In the 16 lap/18 mile Austrailian Pursuit Race Denny Hickey took first place in his Hudson, over Toft and McBride.

## *Mulford Wins Race Before Great Crowd*

Under beautiful skies and before 30,000 people Smiling Ralph Mulford set a track average speed record of 97.24 in the 100 lap 1918 Autumn Classic. Chevrolet, Toft, Duray, Fetterman, and Milton followed. The Frontenac team had a great day finishing first, second, and fourth!

The Italian racer, Resta, competed with Chevrolet and Mulford in the first heat of the match races, but acquired a splinter in his front tire on the death curve, sending him into a tail spin and taking him out of the game. Denny Hickey had a similar accident toward the race's end and skillfully held the car on its wheels, bringing himself and his mechanic out unhurt. Chevrolet had been leading the big race all the way, but a tire change cost him his place.

In the paper discussing this same race they stated, "Whether or not there will be racing here next year is unsettled. Probably not. But plans are already underway to turn the big oval into an aviation field and with the amplification of the aeronautical program of the army there is a likelihood that a flying school may be located here. This would enable the money put into the big plant to function towards winning the war, something its promoters and owners are extremely anxious to do.

Luckily, fighting officially ended November 11, 1918 and racing continued for four more seasons!

National Auto Company was located on Fayette Street in Uniontown.

STANDARD GARAGE

C. W. JOHNSON, OWNER

ARCH AND PETER STREETS

# *Yesteryear At The Uniontown Speedway 1919*

The May 21, 1919 Uniontown newspaper announced:

## *Summit Revels Get Into Local Courts*

Saturday Night's Shindig Likely to get
Three Well Known Local Boys into the Courts

### *Picture Of Devaststion*

"Police court echoes of the exotic revels of Summit night life may soon be reverberating through the halls and sacred cloisters of Uniontown society if the legal steps taken today by Manager Leopold Heyn of the big mountain hotel are pushed to their logical conclusion."

It seems Heyn pressed charges on three young prominent Uniontown fellows who had been partying in town and decided to see what was happening at the Summit Hotel. The spring races had been postponed because of a steady downpour and a ball was being held. The celebration that was scheduled to begin after the races, started early because of the rainy weather. When these three fellows (all of which were veterans of distinguished service in France; two wore honored wound stripes), entered the Summit lobby, it was so crowded they decided to rent a room and party from there.

While they made their way down the long west hall, they found themselves approaching the exclusive headquarters of the famous speed kings where "beverages of proof were said to have been quaffed in mad abandon as sounds of the joyous evening percolated through the big building."

When the men first joined the race car drivers and crews, things went well. They drank toasts to every driver in the Victory Sweepstakes race which was rescheduled for the following Monday. Then they drank to each and every divisional commander in the Allied Forces. No one could pinpoint the actual beginning of the brawl, but to use the statement "all hell broke loose" is quite appropriate here. Mortal combat was waged throughout the entire west wing. Heavy and ponderous blows were exchanged, and one famous automobile owner claimed that he was kicked while he was down-by one of the local intruders. Furniture was destroyed, eyes blackened, ears gouged, lips swelled, and teeth loosened.

The next day Manager Heyn went to the local magistrate, filing charges.. Because the violators were from respected Uniontown families, their names were not used in the paper, but the speed kings were unimpressed with their lack of manners.

### *Puncture At Finish Cost Chevrolet Race*

Louis Chevrolet and Tommy Milton turned the race into a dead heat between them going over 100mph into the 99th lap of the 100 lap Victory Sweepstakes Race when the Frenchman's right rear tire was punctured by a splinter. The explosion was so loud it was easily heard above the trip hammer engines. At this time Chevrolet was a mere 20 feet behind Milton's fabulous

Duesenberg. Many believed he would have passed Milton had the puncture not occurred, but no one will ever know. Mulford took 3rd and the rest of the drivers were way behind the trio. There was never a time in the race when any of the three pros had more than 200 yards on the other, but Milton took the lead in the 55th and was never passed.

In the 95th lap, Chevrolet uncorked the greatest sprint ever seen on the track since opening day when Hughie Hughes went after Chevrolet just before his accident. Milton knew it was do or die as Chevrolet caught him, but then, a splinter caused a tire to explode on the Frontenac.

The scant crowd of 7,000 watched some of the best driving ever witnessed here and had the great pleasure of witnessing the acrobatic work of Lieutenant Locklear. When he stood on the upper wing of the plane and extended his hands they were sailing at a mile a minute. This was the thrill of the day, as the postponement of the race cut the crowd to small proportions and other than a few slight mishaps, it was a quiet, but beautiful day.

All hoped that the upcoming July 19 race would have fine weather as they would hold the close of the big Welcome Home celebration for the returned soldiers of Fayette County.

Racers left Uniontown for Indianapolis where they would run a 300 mile classic on Decoration Day.

Milton took home $3,000.00; Chevrolet, $2,000.00; and Mulford $1,000.00.

## *200 Lap Speedway Race to be Held Here on Labor Day*

After postponing the July 19 race because of continual downpours and drizzle, it was held before a crowd of only 15,000 - 1,500 of which were soldiers there as guests of the management. Milton won both the first and final heats, running the final at an average speed of 101.17mph. Dave Lewis drove his Meteor to second place, tailed by Red Fetterman's Peerless, and Oldfield's Golden Sub driven by Searles.

Judge Frank Rosboro warned Fetterman for jockeying Searles on turns and stretches, but Oldfield filed no complaint. Rain threatened all day, but never spilled over. This threat kept thousands away, and the management proceeded to plan a Labor Day super thrill race.

## *Flames Rob Milton Of Deserved Race Victory*

At the Third Annual Autumn Classic Uniontown Speedway Race, fair weather predominated. For the first time that year, the scheduled race was not postponed because of inclement weather. The last two post-war races saw small crowds, but the Labor Day event was a smashing success. Attendance was estimated at 28,000. Total receipts came to $79,000.00 with speedway profits of $50,000.00. Total motor cars in attendance were close to 6,000.

Frontenacs won three of the top four spots as Joe Boyer grabbed the big money. Roscoe Searles came in 2nd with Chevrolet and Mulford just behind him in their Frontenacs. Then came Dave Lewis, Art Klein, Toland Nichelson, and Wilmer Monahan.

On the 190th lap, Tommy Milton's Duesenberg burst into flames as it left the Death Curve. He turned the car around, moving the flames away from him, and slammed into the inner guard rail. He burnt his hands, feet, and face escaping and tumbled over the rail into the infield as $20,000.00 worth of fine machinery went up in smoke.

Throughout the race Milton out-drove Chevrolet and Mulford, but toward the end Milton was running on 7 cylinders after breaking a connecting rod when one wheel dropped into one of the holes on Death

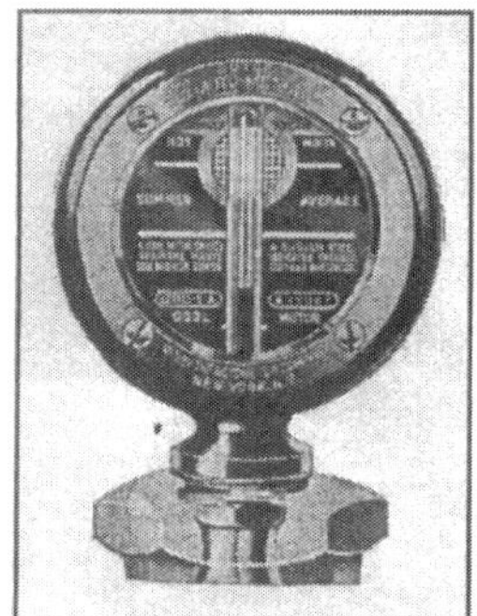



Curve. He knew the risk he was taking, but prayed he could cross the finish line before the race car had all it could stand. The dead cylinder filled with gas. Backfire from the exhaust set the car on fire and Milton's first run was over.

Gaston Chevrolet had been driving the Frontenac that won the race, but was replaced by Joe Boyer when he came into the pits to reshod the Frontenac.

Vivian Prescott, motion picture star and wife of starter Neil Whalen, attracted much attention and was hailed to have the grandest costume among the distinguished in the boxes.

The Braender tire held the best record for endurance as Mulford's set lasted through Sheepshead Bay, Tacoma, and Uniontown.

Milton's mechanic, W.D. Kessler fell in love here and married Miss Gladys Bean of South Beeson Avenue. When he was not on the road, Uniontown was now his home. While Milton and Kessler had their wounds and burns dressed, many of the "fancy" ladies showed their emotions and were quieted down with much difficulty.

It was this year that the wooden track began to deteriorate, boasting holes the size of man holes. Repairs were planned to have the track in ship shape for the spring of 1920.

The track was hailed as the greatest in America.

Milton spent two months in the Uniontown hospital and it is legend that he was quite a flirt with the female employees there, forever flattering and joking with them.

Tommy Milton's Duesenberg #9 caught fire during this race while coming out of "Death's Curve." Milton spent two months in the Uniontown Hospital, where workers say he brightened their days. The man to the left, leaning against car #2 is Ralph Mulford. The car is a Frontenac.

(photo 1) Uniontown Speedway Victory Sweepstakes, Saturday May 17, 1919. Tommy Milton's Duesenberg #9 to the left. Smiling Ralph Mulford second from left. The next is unknown, Augustus Stickel with cigar, Johnny Bresnahan, Frank Eastman, Fred Essig, Omar Toft, E.E. Case, Louis Chevrolet, Pete Henderson, E.V. Goodson, unknown.
(photo 2) Unknown, Joe Thomas, Denny Hickey with striped sleeves, Wilber D'Alene, William Vetere, Tommy Milton in striped shirt, Neil Whalen, starter, with checkered flag, Cliff Durant, unknown, Ernie Ansterberg, Joe Boyer, unknown, Gaston and Arthur Chevrolet.
(photo 3) Robert Bandini, Louis LeCocq, Kurt Hitke, H.E. McGuire, next five unknown, Gus Stickel in cardigan sweater, Smiling Ralph Mulford saluting to far right (half shown).

# PROMINENT DRIVERS USING DIXON'S GRAPHITE AUTOMOBILE LUBRICANTS

DARIO RESTA
"I thank you for the wonderful lubrication given by Dixon's Graphite. I cannot praise it too highly."

THOMAS MILTON
"Say anything you like in my name, I am an enthusiastic user of Dixon's Graphite Automobile Lubricants."

TOM ALLEY
"For a car that receives hard usage I recommend Dixon's Graphite Automobile Lubricants. I do not believe that the other lubricants would give me the same results."

EDDIE HEARNE
"Dependability is the reason I use Dixon's Graphite Automobile Lubricants. I know that I can depend upon every pound to give the best lubrication."

GIL ANDERSON
"All of our notable winnings last year were made while using Dixon's Graphite Automobile Lubricants, which for several seasons have been used by Stutz racing teams."

ORA HAIBE
"I am always willing to go to any amount of trouble to secure Dixon's Graphite Automobile Lubricants."

I. P. FETTERMAN
"Dixon's Graphite Automobile Lubricants will always be a part of my racing equipment. I would rather not drive than have to drive without them."

IRA VAIL
Uses and recommends Dixon's Graphite Automobile Lubricants.

# *Denny Hickey, Dawson Racer*

On April 28, 1909 Denny Hickey, 19, won the Championship Fayette County 13 Mile Marathon Race at Stillwagon-Marietta Park in Connellsville. He was born in Dawson, son of Mr.. and Mrs. Edward Hickey. As a young teenager, he was a friend of Sarah B. Cochran's niece. Mrs. Cochran, wife of Dawson's famed coal and coke baron "Little" Jimmy Cochran, bought herself a car in the early 1900's. At this time she knew no one who had driving skills, but Hickey had been chauffeuring her carriage. Mrs. Cochran's niece suggested that she ask Hickey to learn to drive her new car. She did just that and Hickey proved to be more than up to the task..

In the Memorial Day Indianapolis 500 of 1919, Dawson born Denny Hickey drove the "Stickel" to take 9th place in the first big race to be run after World War I ended. The #59 Hudson, owned by Connellsville Hudson dealer, Augustus Stickel, covered the 500 miles of brick track in 6 hours, 13 minutes, and 57.24 seconds. After 10 (2 1/2 mile per lap) laps, his car moved to 24th place and by the time he ran 80 laps, he had reached 13th place. During the last 10, Hickey gave all the 6 cylinder had and pushed on to make history. His average speed in that race was 80.22mph. Hickey had been trained in the car racing field by Earl Porter and entered in his first races by Burges J. McGill.

As you go through the earlier chapters in this book you will see that Hickey was a contender in many races at the Uniontown Speedway. His love for cars grew, but after 1919, he got married and had a family, hanging up his racing goggles. He opened Hickey's Brake Service on Crawford Avenue in Connellsville January 15, 1926.

Daughters Mary Louise Clemmer and Anne Hickey of Connellsville remember their father as a man with a great sense of humor. A good old boy from the old board track, he taught his children to drive, sold cars, worked as a mechanic, and became foreman for the Fayette County Department of Highways. His life's work involved motor vehicles and he shall always be remembered as Fayette County's own Speed Demon.

Maggie, Pat, and Denny Hickey in the very early 1900's at their Dawson home. Was Hickey dreaming of race cars as a boy?

L - R in the #59 Hudson that Hickey drove in the Indy 500 winning $1,600.00 for eighth place, are: mechanic Pete O'Brien, Denny Hickey, and unknown (standing). The car was owned by Gus Stickel of Connellsville.

# Yesteryear At The Uniontown Speedway 1920

The National Prohibition or "Volstead Act" began midnight January 16, 1920, outlawing intoxicating liquors with an alcohol content over 5%. There were concessions for medicinal, sacramental, and industrial purposes and for fruit and grape beverages made on your own property for home use. Smuggling, distilling, fermentations, and brewing became legend. Speak easies, bootlegging, and organized crime grew rapidly, making the government corrupt at all levels. Prohibition lasted 14 years, during which our Fayette County mountains and foot hills joined in the above mentioned past times with great zeal. Although none of the articles mentioned this, I would say that was the end of selling beer at the Uniontown Speedway, but as you will see, the law did not stand between the people and their thrills.

The Headline of the Daily Standard June 19, 1920 read:

## Speedway Crowd Is Biggest Ever

### Cars And Drivers Are Fit

The morning before the race, papers referred to it as the "longest, classiest, and probably the best automobile race ever run on the Uniontown Speedway." The weather was perfect and advance ticket sales were by far the heaviest in history. Roads were "black with cars" as thousands poured into the city. Street cars were jammed all day long looking like "sardine carriers" and the special trains run from Pittsburgh and all branches in the southwestern area of the state were due in at 1pm full of "speed bugs for the big whirl".

Sixteen cars and drivers were all fit and ready to run with Ralph DePalma having clocked unofficially the night before up to 106mph in a test run. He was reported to have been smiling broadly when seen that night.. Milton and Mulford were the common favorites as fans suspected their cars would hold out longer than the Italian's in the grueling 225 mile/200 lap grind. Gaston Chevrolet, Jimmy Murphy, Roscoe Searles, and I.P. Fetterman were here to show their skill, and Denny Hickey still had his following. Predictions were, that the average speed could be 90mph if the planked surface could stand the horrific strain.

## Milton Holding Victory at Speedway

### But One Smash-up In 225 Mile Speed Card

June 21, 1920 Morning Herald: "Tommy Milton, world's title holding speed pilot, put his second mark on the Universal Trophy cup Saturday afternoon at the Uniontown Speedway by winning the fifth Universal Trophy race, a 225 mile event, making the distance in two hours, twenty-two minutes, forty four and thirty six hundredth seconds at an average of 94.9mph. This was Milton's second consecutive Universal

Trophy. If he wins the next one it is his to keep permanently.

Murphy, O'Donnell, and Fetterman followed the winner marking the first time in history for a team (Duesenberg) of drivers to take all top spots. Cash prizes were $5,000.00 for 1st, $3,000.00 for 2nd, $2,000.00 3rd, $1,500.00 4th. Ralph Mulford, Benny Hill, Joe Thomas, and Roscoe Searles finished in that order for $1,000.00, $750.00. $500.00, and $250.00.

Fifty thousand race fans witnessed as Wade Day Morton rounded the Death Curve on the 180th lap, turned a somersault, and rested against the guard rail. Mechanician Arthur Kaemp was thrown clear of the wreck and into the soft soil of the infield. Morton was held in his seat by the steering wheel. Kaemp was taken to the hospital and treated for brush burns, but both fellows faired uninjured otherwise.

After the first hundred laps Gaston Chevrolet and Roscoe Searles were sure contenders for first place, but during the 118th, Chevrolet retired his Frontenac because of a "wounded engine." Searles, driving a Monroe for Louis Chevrolet went to the pits in the 119th, but the time lost giving the machine a "once-over" cost him his spot at the top. Art Klein's engine "gasped for breath and died" when he was 200 yards from the tape, 7th place his by 2 laps. This is funny today, but I assume it was not amusing to the men at the time, as the mechanic (with numb legs from the long hard ride) tried his best to dash to the pits for a can of gas as Klein attempted to push the Frontenac to the finish. As this scene progressed, Joe Thomas passed them and took their coveted prize.

I.P."Red" Fetterman took 4th place by running the 200 lap race at a steady pace of 91mph with no stops. Joe Thomas lost 4th place to Fetterman when he ran out of gas on Death's Curve. When he returned to the track, Searle was in the same predicament. During the 159th lap, the fastest pit work in the history of the track was set when Milton's crew changed his tire in nine seconds.

Before the Autumn Classic of 1919, the race days at the speedway consisted of not only the two main races, but several heats and championships. Last year's 225 mile race proved to the management that spectators wanted the big races for the big money and that is what they intended to offer. For the first time in the speedway's history, the grand stand was filled to total capacity. There was not a seat left to be had. Uniontown had never known such crowds in the history of its life. Estimated profits for the Uniontown Speedway Association was estimated at $90,000.00 with estimated receipts at $125,000.00.

At this point, the wooden track was filling radiators and injuring drivers with splinters. The half of the track used most needed resurfacing badly and it was estimated the work would take $100,000.00 and a full two months of labor. Both Ralph DePalma and Tommy Milton suffered cuts and sores from the flying wooden pieces, DePalma's stuck behind his elbow. Drivers left town a few days after the race, heading to Tacoma for the July 5th extravaganza. They were assured by speedway officials that if the track did not get a complete working over, it would definitely be more than adequately repaired for the next big race.

After the race, 126 boy scouts were on hand to direct the heavy traffic and help assure safety to fans. "All roads led to the Summit" after the race as a victory party ensued to celebrate the greatest day of the Uniontown Speedway thus far.

Out of the twelve races held there at that time, eight had been postponed because of rain. The speedway association began insuring the weather with Chisholm & Kunkle who would have paid the association $30,000.00 if it had rained for the race. This seemed to work, for the rain ceased and all went well.

The headline September 7, 1920 read:

## *Milton Wins Speedway Crown Before Local Crowd*

Papers reported that a record breaking crowd packed the speedway for 1920's Autumn Classic. Milton gave his fans a show cracking the track record by averaging 96mph in his mighty Duesenberg, There were no injuries, and the tree limbs that usually blocked the score board were bare.

By winning this 225 mile race, Milton fixed himself as number one among American speedway drivers. Gaston Chevrolet came right behind him with his May 1920 Indy 500 win. Milton, Murphy, and O'Donnell ran the first hundred laps as if their Duesenbergs were tied together with a string. Hearne was thought to be the fastest driver of the day and if he was not forced into pit stops so often, would have taken the money. Gaston Chevrolet was ridiculed when he side- swiped Waldo Stein's Monroe toward the end of the race. Stein finished the race minus his right brake band which he lost in the crash.

Positions, cars, and prizes were as follows at the finish:

1st, Milton, Duesenberg, $5,000.00; 2nd, Murphy, Duesenberg, $3,000.00; 3rd, Hearne, Revere-Duesenberg, $2,000.00; 4th, O'Donnell, Duesenberg, $1,500.00; 5th, Chevrolet, Monroe, $1,000.00; 6th, Miller, Duesenberg, $750.00; 7th, Stein, Frontenac, $750.00. Ralph DePalma was put out of the race the day before because of a broken piston. The Italian speed king has had a run of bad luck at the Uniontown track from the beginning.

Milton had been working on a new race car and promised crowds that he would be running his Duesenberg motor on a Frontenac chasis the following year. "Watch me next year," he told them.

June 19, 1920, Eddie O'Donnell's #9 Duesenberg. He took 3rd place this day.

June 19, 1920, Cars L - R are: #3 Joe Thomas, Monroe Frontenac; Ernie Ansterberg's #5 Monroe Frontenac, Art Klein, #8 Frontenac; Winner Tommy Milton's #10 Duesenberg.

1920 Uniontown Speedway Action. Mr. and Mrs. Jess Kyler and Mrs. Bert McCartney (mother of the late Adelaide Wolfe of Ohiopyle) enjoying a day at the races.

# Yesteryear at the Uniontown Speedway 1921

## Big Farm Power Test at Speedway Monday

Almost 2,000 people from southwestern Pennsylvania, Maryland, and West Virginia were guests of Henry Ford and 22 Allied Ford dealers in the northeastern United States for the first combined demonstration of farming machinery ever held in Fayette County, May 23, 1921. Farming motorists from all around came to view and test every kind of farm equipment that had yet been invented to aid in crop growing..

Four railroad cars of equipment was shipped from Washington, Pennsylvania, where Ford had held a similar demonstration. This included plows, harrows, discs, thrushers, saw mills, stone crushers, pulverizers, feed grinders, shredders, hay bailers, and corn pickers. There were more than fifteen companies represented in addition to the Ford Motor Compny with its Fordson Tractors.

The demonstration began at 9am with a dinner being served free of charge to all on the grounds at noon.

At this time tickets were being sold for the Universal race coming up in June. A full row of box seats had been added to the covered section of the grand stand.

## Mulford Breaks All Records In Page Stock "6"

Under official sanction and supervision, Smiling Ralph Mulford drove his Paige Cat to break records for the 5, 10, 15, 20, 25, 50, 75, and 100 mile marks May 20, 1921 at the Uniontown Speedway. The Crichton Timing System was used as it was regarded as the best. Representing the A.A.A. were G.E. Edwards, chairman of the technical committee; A.H. Means, secretary of the contest board; and F.H. Rosboro, Uniontown Speedway Association board representative.

Mulford's trial was devoid of thrills other than his right rear tire burning off about halfway through the day. Other than that Mulford displayed the utmost skill with his driving. It was said then, that every Paige on the showroom floors could run as well - all that was needed was a Mulford to tune the motor and be behind the wheel. After breaking all those records, the Paige Cat qualified as the speed champion and the handsomest car in America. They were made by Santos.

The headlines for the sixth annual Universal Trophy Race Saturday, June 18, 1921 read:

## Big Crowd Here For Great Race

### Milton Rules As Favorite

Under overcast skies, thousands poured into Uniontown as ticket sales broke records. The crowd was so intense that special traffic rules were put in force by local police as follows:

Fayette Street from the intersection of Morgantown and Fayette Streets, was open to east bound traffic only on race day from 11am to 2pm.

The National Pike was closed to west bound traffic during the same hours between the W.A. Stone home and the Fayette/Morgantown Street intersection. Autos traveling west were diverted at the Stone home to the Country Club Road. The Derrick Avenue route to the track was closed to east bound traffic at the Barton Mill Road from 11am to 2pm. No cars were permitted further east than the Barton Mill Road.

Talk among the fans was that Milton's Frontenac had a new cylinder block that was not yet broken in and the car had just arrived the night before. Milton had won the Indy 500 the past Memorial Day with a new block which had only 30 miles on it, so bets were going his way. The odds were: Milton, even money to win; Murphy 1 to 2; Hearne 1 to 3; Sealres 1 to 3; and Mulford 1 to 4.

Hotels and restaurants were swamped both in town and the mountains, but by now were well prepared for race crowds and gladly served them. One well known but unidentified establishment baked 900 loaves of 25 slice bread for the day. Over 50,000 meals would easily be served in the city throughout the day.

An after race banquet was planned at the Summit Hotel where crowds would throng immediately to take a dip in the pool and get some relief from the heat and humidity. A 100 seat dinner was served to drivers, mechanics, pit crews, A.A.A. officials, and Speedway Association directors at 9pm with the usual dance following.

The race's weather was insured by Lloyd's of London, through Chisholm & Kunkle and the race could only be called off by the insurance company fifteen minutes before the scheduled events.

At this time, the Volstead Act had not yet been passed. Some were trying to change a section of the bill making it possible to have beer prescribed as medicine. This did not go over as it was assumed physicians would be swamped with the "ill".

Neil Whalen was the starter and Frank Rosboro referee for the 200 lap/225 mile race. Frontenacs were driven by Thomas Milton, Ralph Mulford, Jules Ellingboe, Allon Soules, and Joe Thomas. Wonderlich, Jimmie Murphy, Roscoe Searles, and Eddie Miller ran Duesenbergs. Frank Elliot was in a Leach Special and Eddie Hearne went for the money in a Revere Special.

## *Searles in Duesenberg wins Universal Race*

Searles "smashed through to victory with the greatest burst of sustained speed ever registered on the local track." His #6 Duesie was Milton's #10 from the year before. His time for top money was two hours, eighteen minutes and 19:42 seconds, stopping just once to adjust a disconnected spark plug. If it had not been for that one stop, Searles' average speed of 97.75 mph would have broke 100mph. Top prize was $5,000.00 and possession of the Universal Trophy. He had qualified at 101.4mph.

Eddie Hearne came in 2nd in his Revere; Eddie Miller took 3rd in his Duesenberg; Tommy Alley came in 4th in a Frontenac. Tommy Milton took eighth place . It was said that the only man happier than Fred and Augie Duesenberg that day was Mack Rush of the Motor Square Garage. Mack handled both the Duesenberg and the Revere.

Only one accident occurred throughout the day. In lap 128 a broken steering knuckle caused Chicago's Jules Ellingboe's Frontenac to take a terrific spill at the start of the north turn close to the National Pike. The racer swerved into the inside guard rail, leaped over the six foot bank into the infield, spun around twice, ran back onto the track, and finally collapsed on the inside apron. Ellingboe and mechanic Wallace Butler were thrown from the car causing them serious, but not fatal, injuries.

By this time most cars were using Oldfield (Firestone) tires, whose high quality kept racers on the track and away from the pits for tire changes. A record low of three tire changes was set at the speedway this day. One dangerous hole developed along the outside edge of the straightaway, just in front of the first section of the grand stand. Neil Whalen had a time steering drivers away from the hole.

Because of the threat of rain, attendance was healthy, but under par compared to the Autumn Classic of 1920. After the race, the mountain was packed with cars up and down the pike, along Jumonville Road, and the Summit parking lot had over 300 autos there! Seventeen extra state policemen were on hand to control additional traffic.

An hour after the race, a shower ensued and Lloyds of London was in the clear. Just after the rain a West Virginia Essex (Major Jimmy Miller of Wheeling) and a Uniontown Ford worked their way onto the track from the infield and began tearing around the track at top speed. On his fourth lap, Miller was flying past the grand stand when he attempted to climb the steep embankment on the north curve up to the white line. To do this a car had to be going a solid 85mph to stick. The Essex began sliding sideways on the wet boards going into a spill, turning two circles, and finally crashed into the lower guard rail. The Major was merely surprised, but the poor Essex was badly damaged.

The Ford who was nameless in the newspapers, did the identical stunt and landed close to Miller. The thousand or so fans who still remained at the track, had a good laugh and the mystery still remains on how the fellows escaped injury.

## *Fetterman Takes Top Spot Labor Day*

It seemed that this was a strange race. Tommy Milton drove a Frontenac and Roscoe Searles was behind the wheel of Milton's Leach Miller. Later in the race the Frontenac went to the pits permanently and Milton drove relief for Hearne in his Disteel-Duesie and put on "a spectacular display of driving."

Searles averaged 103mph for the first seven miles of the 225 mile race. Tire wear prevented Jimmy Murphy from winning when he and Fetterman were in a heated duel as were Searles and Milton. Howdy Wilcox, protégé of Louis Chevrolet, was hanging with the leaders the first hundred laps. During private trials days before, he had clocked 7mph faster than Milton. In the 89th lap he went to the pits with a flat, telling Chevrolet he was going to "cut loose then and there". On his third lap he was clocked at 105mph and was on the verge of jumping to the lead when Murphy and Searles went in for tire changes.

Just then Joe Thomas in his Duesie #5 skidded off the top boards coming out of the north turn and spun around in the direct path of Wilcox's Frontenac. When Thomas was thrown out of the car, Wilcox went through the barrier backwards from jamming on his emergency brake to miss hitting the man and the car. He got turned back around in the infield and broke through the rails on the other side of the track front forward. None of the men were injured. Pates Boyle, a Uniontown man who wanted to taste speedway thrills and compare them with his aviation experiences, was riding with Wilcox. He commented that it was easier to ride the clouds of Germany or the waves of the

Atlantic in a fast motorboat, than the jarring hillocks of the local track.

Red Fetterman, Pittsburgh's new speedway race star, was approached by two of the largest financial backers in the racing game later that evening at the Summit Hotel. They told him that he was assured all the support money could buy for the 1922 season.

Estimated profits for the race were $25,000.00.

Stands were packed and no one knew that this would be one of the last races held at the famous board track, September 5, 1921.

Unknown Uniontown Speedway racer.

**Quality is the Best.**

The inside of this Speedway program of 10,000 copies, containing thirty-two pages and binding, was printed and bound within five days time and ready for delivery. With its Meihle press and self-feeding Miller job press, with a speed of 2500 per hour, and three other job presses and linotype machine, and hundreds of fonts of job type faces, The Uniontown Printing Company is the best equipped job office in the county. For speed and first-class work they can't be equaled. Give them a trial and satisfy yourself.

**The Old Record Bldg., 81 S. Beeson Ave.
Uniontown, Pa.**

SEVERAL REBUILT

# Racing Roadsters

Can be used for pleasure with the knowledge that you can pass the "other fellow" on the level or on the steepest hill. Also suitable for dirt track racing.

C. E. FISHER

Care of Jay Bee Stands at Speedway
or J. B. Co., Uniontown, Pa.

This photo has no date, but may be a smaller race held for locals. Denny Hickey is the sixth man from the left and Red Fetterman is five men to his left.

Charlie Johnson stands to the far right of the row.

# *Yesteryear at the Uniontown Speedway - 1922*

## *Racing Drivers Tell Radio Fans About Big Race*

The week of June 11 - 15, 1922 marked the first time in history that racing drivers talked to their fans via radio. The broadcast was staged at the Pittsburgh Post studio of the Westinghouse KDKA station in Pittsburgh. World famous race stars who were entered to drive in the June 16, seventh annual Universal Trophy cup race entertained with their stories and predictions.

I.P. "Red" Fetterman, Pittsburgh native and winner of the 1921 Autumn Classic, was lead on man. Tommy Milton told thousands of fans that he was about to run the most difficult race of his career on the Uniontown track. Harry Harris, Jimmy Murphy, and the master of them all, Barney Oldfield, kept the "listeners in" close to their radios.

## *Federal Court Issues Injunction Restraining Brownfield Interference with Races*

It was reported that the June 17, 1922 Universal Trophy cup race would be cancelled. The Uniontown Speedway Association had declared bankruptcy and the last race had been backed financially by Pittsburgh car dealer and Uniontown Speedway Association Vice President, Frank D. Saupp. Since so many of the races through the years had been postponed because of rain, most of the crowd that would come to town for the big race had to leave, and days later when the race would be run, profits were low because of their bad luck. Although they had planned to redo the track, this never happened as funds were not up to expectations.

Mrs. Mary Brownfield, owner of the land where the speedway was built, requested an injunction from the local courts against the defunct speedway association on grounds of default. Luckily the speedway association had filed for an injunction of their own. They slapped the Mr.. and Mrs. I.H. Brownfield with a restraining order disallowing their interference with the big race. This was the day before the race and drivers were relieved to get their cars on the track for qualifications and test drives before competing the next day. Mr.. Brownfield had gone to the track the day before, disrupting workmen and ordering everyone off of the premises. The speedway association was then operating under a lease from their attorney, Dean Stugis.

Ticket sales were going well, but the track itself was still in need of major repair. There were fourteen entries for the Universal Trophy cup 225 lap race. In addition to the $3,000.00 trophy, $12,000.00 in cash and accessory prizes were offered. Five new drivers were to run their first race this day. Harry Hartz, who came in 2nd behind Jimmy Murphy in that year's Indy 500, was here to run this track for the first time, also. He had watched many speed shows at the famous track and was looking forward to trying out the boards.

Jimmy Murphy led qualifications with 109.46mph. Tommy Milton registered 108.26, and four others ran their laps at over 100mph. They were: Frank Elliot, 106mph; Harry Hartz, 105 1/2mph; Jerry Wonderlich and I.P. Fetterman ran at 101 1/4mph. To get those speeds in one lap is doing some on a track that was then littered with holes and splintered. To do 200 laps on wood in that kind of shape took nerve and skill.

Murphy's time was a track record. He had his start as a driver here and was not aware that his would be the standing record that would go down in history (and into a book called Yesteryear at the Uniontown Speedway). The weatherman called for rain throughout the day, but fans were in place and drivers ready to go.

# *Murphy Wins Big Race*

## *New Records on Local Speedway in Big Event*

Hartz, Elliot, and Milton Eliminated after many Thrilling Speed Brushes
Two in Non-Stop Runs
They came in like this.

1. Jimmy Murphy, Miller-Dues. (Murphy Special)
2. Ralph Mulford, Frontenac
3. Jerry Wonderlich, Duusenberg
4. I.P. Fetterman, Duesenberg
5. Ora Haibe, Frontenac
6. Harlan Fengler, Miller
7. Arthur Chevrolet, Frontenac
8. Ernie Olsen, Duesenberg
9. Benny Hill, Miller
10. Harry Hartz, Duesenberg
11. Tommy Milton, Leach-Miller
12. Frank Elliot, Leach-Miller
13. Leon Duray,Frontenac

Jimmy Murphy set yet another track record at the last race run on the old board track. His average speed was 102.2 for $5,000.00. Mulford took 2nd with an average speed of 100.75mph and Wonderlich took 3rd with a speed of 100.25. Murphy took the lead in the 114th lap from Hartz, when the latter was forced into the pits for a tire change. The Los Angeles driver kept that lead until he piloted his Murphy Special across the finish line a full two laps in front of Mulford. He had such a great run going, the speed pilot drove his racer a full extra lap after Neil Whalen flagged him at the finish.

During the 72nd lap, Milton was leading the race with an average speed of 101 1/2mph. He then went through the lower guard rail at the precise spot where his car burned three years before, putting him in the hospital with severe burns for two months. This time he was much luckier. Coming out of Death Curve his right rear wheel collapsed and was thrown across the track, landing under the grand stand within inches of the spectators seated there. The tail of the Leach Special was smashed and axles bent, but Milton and mechanic, George Steel, came out smiling and waving to 10,000 screaming fans. As Milton's big grey car rammed its tail into a locust post of the guard rail, Starter Neil Whalen said, "I have seen a lot of accidents, but that is about the luckiest"

Hartz then took the lead until the 114th lap when Murphy showed no mercy. Hartz again returned to the pits in the 166th lap, this time to repair a broken oil line, and Murphy took the race from there with record breaking speed. Smiling Ralph Mulford paced himself throughout the race and made only one pit stop. As drivers beat their cars at extreme speed, Mulford hung tight, slowly moving into that runner-up position. Fetterman and Wonderlich both drove non stop for 225 miles. Although Fetterman all but fainted during the last 30 laps, his mechanic did some gymnastic driving to bring the Pittsburgh driver into the money for $1,000.00.

The threat of rain again kept spectators away and a mere 10,000 folks cheered the stars on to their victory. The intake of cash obviously did not put the speedway association in the money, and even though Frank D. Saupp assured the press that an Autumn Classic would be held that year, none was.

## *Speedway Will Collect $2,500 Rain Insurance*

Because it rained in Wheeling the day of the race and their insurance policy stated that it could not rain in Uniontown, Pittsburgh, Cumberland, Fairmont, and Wheeling, a check was issued in payment from the Lloyds Insurance Company.

It was rumored that Charlie Johnson, President of the Uniontown Speedway, took off with the proceeds of the last race and went to a southern country to retire. I have found no proof to that effect and am here to help clear his name. The Uniontown Speedway Association was in financial trouble and there was little money to be had. Johnson was a respected Buick dealer and was not financially (as far as I know) dependent on the track to support him. The late Neal Wood of Connellsville, who had worked in the entertainment field and "handled" the track, said in a Tribune Review interview in 1980 that monies were deposited by Treasurer R.M. "Bob" Sample immediately after each race in the Union Trust Bank and rumors that management took the money and ran, were untrue. Further evidence supports this as you will read that Charlie Johnson spoke before the opening race at the New Uniontown Speedway in 1940.

## *Fire Destroys Coast Speedway*

San Carlos Track Burned With Loss Estimated at $200,000.

The day after the last race here, the greater San Francisco Speedway Boardtrack in San Carlos, California burnt.

It seems the era of wooden tracks was coming to an end.

June 17, 1922. This was the final race run at the old board track. From L - R: Unknown, Dwight Kessler, George Stiehl, H.S. McKee, Harlen Fengler, Tommy Milton, Harry Hartz, Ernie Olson, Gus Stickel, Frank Elliot, next two unknown, Jimmy Henderson, M. Treyvoux.

June 17, 1922 - Arthur Chevrolet, Steve Nemish, C.G. Howard, unknown, Leon Duray, Louis Chevrolet, next two unknown, Smiling Ralph Mulford, Ira Vail, Augie Duesenberg, Ora Haibe, Shorty Hansen, Dario Resta, Tom Rooney, unknown.

We Insure Anything Against Everything

**$40,000.00 if it Rains**

That's the Amount of the Uniontown Speedway Association Rain Policy for this Race

**CHISHOLM and KUNKLE**

INSURANCE OF ALL KINDS

Real Estate and Coal Lands We will even Loan You a Home

203-4-5-6 Union Trust Building, UNIONTOWN, PA.

We Insure Anything Against Everything

104

"Lone Racer" at the board track. (top left)
Tommy Milton at the Indianapolis, Indiana track (bottom left)
Who owned the Speed Spook? Charlie Johnson? Who is M.A. Lafayette? (top right)

One of the last gatherings at the first Uniontown Speedway, 1922.

# *Studebaker Breaks Records on Summit Mountain*

On May 28, 1928 A.B. Jenkins drove a factory stock Studebaker Commander up the Summit Mountain, cresting the top at 60mph. Jenkins was a famous driver on board and brick tracks, who hired himself out to automobile manufacturers. It was a test drive to prove the Studebaker was the best the country had to offer and the run was considered to be absolutely successful.

Motor critics had given the Summit Mountain national recognition as a proving ground for a car's climbing ability. The Commander was a new mid-size weighing 3,560 pounds. It was a large six cylinder for that day and "low geared". For a cost of $1,495.00 you could purchase this all steel bodied five passenger sedan that offered upholstery of mohair, Gabriel shocks, a speedometer, stop light, windshield wiper, and gas gauge.

The Studebaker had only 37 miles on it and was supplied by the Pittsburgh Studebaker distributor. It was 4 o'clock in the morning. Pittsburgh newspaper editors were on hand to help with the timing while they took notes for their stories. Uniontown mayor, Luther S. Crawford, a Studebaker owner, also served as timer. Officer Corbin-Brown, a Pittsburgh motorcycle patrolman, checked the speedometer.

Jenkins' run began with a flying start at the Watering Trough hauling one passenger. They flew by the Summit Hotel at 60mph. On the second run, he took four reporters with him and topped the hill at 54mph. Fourteen men climbed in and on the Commander and held fast to the sides for the third pull. Hauling this extra 2,346 pounds, the Studebaker showed no strain going over the top at 31mph.

The *Morning Herald* described Jenkins' run as "almost incredible speed". This was considered to be one of the toughest drives in the eastern United States. "No orchestra music ever sounded sweeter to the Studebaker representatives than the hum of the motor in the crisp air of the mountain as the Commander leaped its way into the limelight of motor fame," they stated.

Some of the men who attended this record breaking test drive were: H.E. Jordan, assistant advertising manager from South Bend, Indiana; A.E. Richmond, Pittsburgh Studebaker manager; E.R. Preble, assistant sales director for Pennzoil of Oil City; J.J. Fox, Penzoil's general sales manager; E.E. Parrock, Pittsburgh Studebaker factory representative, H.W. Dietrich, Pittsburgh's Sun Telegraph automobile editor, Allen C. Rankin of the Pittsburgh Press, and the Post Gazette's U.M. Manning.

# Yesteryear at the New Uniontown Speedway 1940

The half mile dirt race track built by the Bryson brothers of Uniontown in 1940 had asphalt turns. They had the unlimited support of the public and all were proud that the Brysons showed such confidence in the area. By investing thousands of dollars in the track, the Oldsmobile, Cadillac, and Diamond T Truck dealers of Uniontown continued Uniontown's imprint on the development of motor cars nationally. This track was built on the same property as the famous wooden track but it faced the opposite direction.

The best racing programs available were being planned with the assurance of long-time continuation. After an eighteen year lapse, Uniontown was filled with the excitement of racing once again.

Qualifying Runs Start at 11am Memorial Day

Uniontown's May 23, 1940 *Morning Herald* stated that a total of twenty two cars had already entered the championship qualifications and ten to fifteen more were expected. The track was scheduled to open at 10am on Memorial Day and at 11am until late that afternoon the dirt track circuit speed kings were to warm up their mounts for a four sprint series which would have proceeded the 50 lap feature attraction. To qualify, each driver had to run three laps. The first two were in reduced speed and the third they were to step on the gas and prove their car's ability to stand the strain of the 25 mile race. The main race was to start at 2:30pm to compete for prize money and CSRA rating list points.

The track was ready and men from ten states lined up to test their skills. The Frontenac and a Miller Special were the only familiar car names from the earlier track. Many of the entries had driven around the country including Indianapolis. The races were rained out. It seemed like an omen from the past as the old speedway had at least eight of their races postponed because of rain. The June 2 race was also called because of weather and an Independence Day race was planned.

The July 5, 1940 headline of the *Morning Herald* read:

## New Speedway Fastest in America

### But One Accident of Minor Nature Occurs to Mar Opening Event

Proof that Charlie Johnson, Uniontown Speedway President from 1916 - 1922, did not "take the money and run" as rumored: He spoke to fans before the 1940 opening race in honor of the track's dedication!

It was decided to run a feature race of thirty instead of fifty laps in order to break the track in. Twelve thousand fans gathered in the grand stand for the opening race of the New Uniontown Speedway. In the first heat the only accident of the day occurred. Elbert Booker of Detroit came roaring into the last lap approaching the judge's stand. At that moment he broke a connecting rod and a large chunk of hot metal flew right at the judges. It just missed veteran starter Henry F. "Hank" Miller and dropped onto the bench next to Sam Nunis who operated the microphone. This put Booker's car out of the race, but he later drove Johnnie Crone's car in a special eight lap feature. Miller had to jump out of the way several times throughout the day to avoid being hit by drivers roaring down the home stretch.

Central States Racing Association champion for 1938 and 1939, Jimmy Wilburn of Los Angeles, brought his Offenhauser across the finish line setting a track record of 11:49:98 for the thirty lap feature. During qualifications, he broke his own world's half mile dirt track record of 21:578 with a time of 21:54. Ed Zaluckle of Detroit and Johnny DeCamp of Richmond, Indiana tied for second.

The races and winners were as follows:

| Car # | Driver | Car | Address | Time |
|---|---|---|---|---|
| | | First Heat - 10 Laps | | |
| 39 | Jimmy Wilburn | Offenhauser | Los Angeles | 3:53.97 |
| 12 | Johnny Crone | Miller Special | Marysville, MD | |
| 2 | Eddie Zaluckle | Dreyer Special | Detroit | |
| | | Second Heat - 10 Laps | | |
| 3 | Johnnie DeCamp | Miller Special | Richmond, Ind. | 4:47 |
| 404 | Bob Garringer | Merkle Special | Denver, CO | |
| 25 | Charles Engle | Engle Special | Dayton, OH | |
| | | Third Heat - 10 Laps | | |
| 15 | Cecil Burnaugher | Gerber Special | Moline, Ill | 4:06.27 |
| 75 | Jack Jiarusso | Miller Special | Pittsburgh | |
| 8 | Harry Schlosser | Hisso | Cincinnati | |
| | | Fourth Heat - 10 Laps | | |
| 7 | Spider Webb | Vance Special | South Gate, CA | 4:07.97 |
| 32 | Whitey Flickinger | Hal Special | Sebring, OH | |
| 11 | Woody Woodford | Dreyer Special | Los Angeles, CA | |
| | | Final Race - 30 Laps | | |
| 39 | Jimmy Wilburn | | | 11:49.98 |
| 3 | Johnny DeCamp | | | |
| 2 | Eddie Zaluckle | | | |
| 7 | Spider Webb | | | |
| 404 | Bob Garringer | | | |
| 25 | Charles Engle | | | |
| 11 | Woody Woodford | | | |
| 8 | Henry Schlosser | | | |
| | | Special Race - 8 Laps | | |
| 8 | Johnny DeCamp | | | 3:06.44 |
| 7 | Spider Webb | | | |
| 2 | Eddie Zaluckle | | | |

Wilburn took the lead from the start of the big race with DeCamp giving him a battle in the first two laps. After that he wound up his machine and pulled out in front of the field of speed demons crossing the finish line to win $650.00. He lapped Spears on the last lap. Spears was the last car. Webb and Schakelford were pelted with stones from the track and forced to retire early during the second heat.

# Donald Zack Winner of Soapbox Derby Class A, Van Swearingen Class B

Uniontown's American Legion used to hold annual Fourth of July Soap Box Derbies on Morgantown Hill. During the race in 1940, fifteen year old Donald Zack, son of Constable and Mrs. Charles Zack, took his victory in style. The year before, his older brother Jimmy took the honors. Chief A.W. Davis was general chairman of the event and the city police force kept the fans off the street for the race. Zack won a place in the National fall soap box derby classic in Akron, Ohio.

The day was ended with a fireworks display at Craig Field where most of the five thousand fans watched the scintillating show.

# Memorial Day Classic 1941

In the program put out by the Brysons for the May 30, 1941 race, the following officials and track personnel were listed:

## Officials of Uniontown Speedway

Clyde Bryson, President; Earl Moser, Secretary-Treasurer; Matty Bain, Business Manager; Robert Clifford, President Judge; Julius Levy, Judge.

## Central States Racing Association Officials

Harry Gilchrist, Representative in Charge; Robert Martindale, Contest Board Chairman; Norman Witte, Secretary of Contest Board; Rook Bruhn, Contest Board Steward; "Happy" Clark, Contest Board Steward; Howdy Wilcox, Official Starter (Wilcox was Louis Chevrolet's driver toward the end of the old boardtrack races.)

## Track Personnel

Wilber "Pat" Monaghan, Race Manager; Sam Nunis, Narrator; Paul Shively, Chief Timer; Dick Hollywood, Scorer; The Henney Co., Ambulance Service; Dr. E.T. Gruetzner, First Aid Supervisor; Miss Charlotte Caton, Registered Nurse; Wrecker Service, Bryson Motor Co. and Duff Axle Co.

The Bryson's New Uniontown Speedway ran through 1947.

Charles Engle at the New Uniontown Speedway

The New Uniontown Speedway opened in 1941, but this photo is believed to be a 1947 race.

Uniontown Speedway
THE CAR Ahead! IT'S OLDSMOBILE
Memorial Day Classic
Friday, May 30, 1941
—PRICE—
15¢
DO NOT PAY ANY MORE!
Oldsmobile
Cadillac
Diamond T Truck
ALWAYS GOOD USED CARS
GENERAL REPAIRS
Bryson Motors
UNIONTOWN, PA.

# The Summit Hotel

**ATOP MT. SUMMIT**

5 Minutes Ride from Speedway

You are cordially invited to visit and inspect this beautiful Resort and all of its facilities, while attending the Races:—

**The Summit Lido Pool and Cabana Beach**

**The Baron Manchhausen Room and Its . . .**
**Nightly Floor Shows and Dances–No Cover**

**The Summit Golf Club and Its Superb**
**Club House and Golf Course**

**The Bamboo Room serving famous and Delicious Food**

**The Pine Terrace, Our Afternoon Cocktail Lounge**

**All Summer and Winter Sports—Open All Year**

The most progressive and most successful Resort in Pennsylvania.
Unsurpassed Climate Magnificent Scenery. No Hayfever—No Asthma.

**Leo Heyn, President**
**Summit Hotel, Inc.**

# *Uniontown Coal Barons 1947 - 1948*

In a 1948 album written and edited for the Uniontown Coal Baron Baseball Team, WMBS Sports Director Jimmy Gismondi describes their two year history as "packed with color, thrills, and heartaches."

The ball team was created in 1947 because of luck and hard work. The Uniontown newspaper had reported that New Castle and Vandergrift were joining the Middle Atlantic Baseball League. Athletes and sportsmen around Uniontown began talking seriously about getting in the league, but all eight slots were filled. Within two months, New Castle sponsors withdrew their investments during a dispute over their baseball field.

The circuit's president was Elmer Daily. He knew of Uniontown's desire to join the league, but worried that it was much too late in the season to begin. They had under two months to prepare for spring training and Daily knew they needed six months.

In a meeting at the White Swan Hotel, Daily spoke with Uniontown's Harry Isabel, Joseph Petko, and Charles P. Yezbak. The Uniontown Baseball Club met each of Daily's doubts and arguments with determined optimism. Local coal barons and business men commenced to put their money together and draw plans to convert the Uniontown Speedway into a Middle Atlantic Minor League Ball Park.

A monumental task, much like that Charlie Johnson faced in 1916 when he had two months to build the Uniontown Speedway boardtrack on this same property, commenced in a flurry. A diamond was laid out, grand stands repaired, and a $20,000.00 lighting system, installed. Grading began and continued daily until the first game.

Their first year was not a great one, tying Johnstown for seventh place. Attendance was third best in the league. In 1948 they spent much of the season winning, but never played again on this particular piece of property which had seen more of Fayette County's sports history than any other acreage until white water rafting hit Ohiopyle in the 1960's.

Some of the stockholders in the Coal Baron team were Joseph Rehanek, Harold "Dutch" Wandel, and Pete Yezbak.

The Middle Atlantic League was created by Pittsburgh newspaperman, Dick Guy and Cumberland, Maryland sportsman Jimmy McGuire in 1925. The next year McGuire owned a Uniontown team that went defunct after one season and dropped out of the league. It was this year that Elmer M. Daily became president and his perseverance is attributed to the fact that 28 cities had played in the league in 20 years.

In 1928, Scottdale's Russell Hockenberry was elected secretary and endeared himself to radio and newspaper reporters. Promoting the games kept the league popular until they suspended operations in 1943 because of the war. The league resumed with six cities in 1946 and eight the next year.

In 1948 the following teams played in this league: Uniontown Coal Barons, Pittsburgh Pirates, Vandergrift Pioneers, Philadelphia Philles, Erie Sailors, New York Giants, Johnstown Johnnies, Brooklyn Dodgers, Butler Yanks, New York Yanks, Oil City Refiners, Chicago White Sox, Youngstown Colts, independent; and the independent New Castle Chiefs. (Farm affiliations included.)

UNIONTOWN
COAL
BARONS
1948
SOUVENIR ALBUM
$1.50

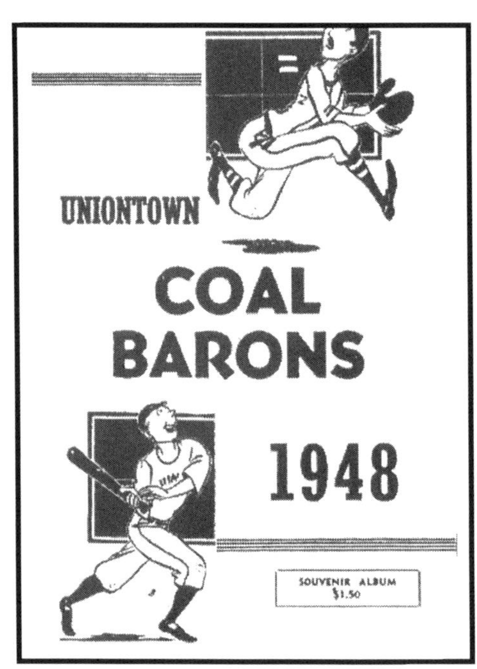

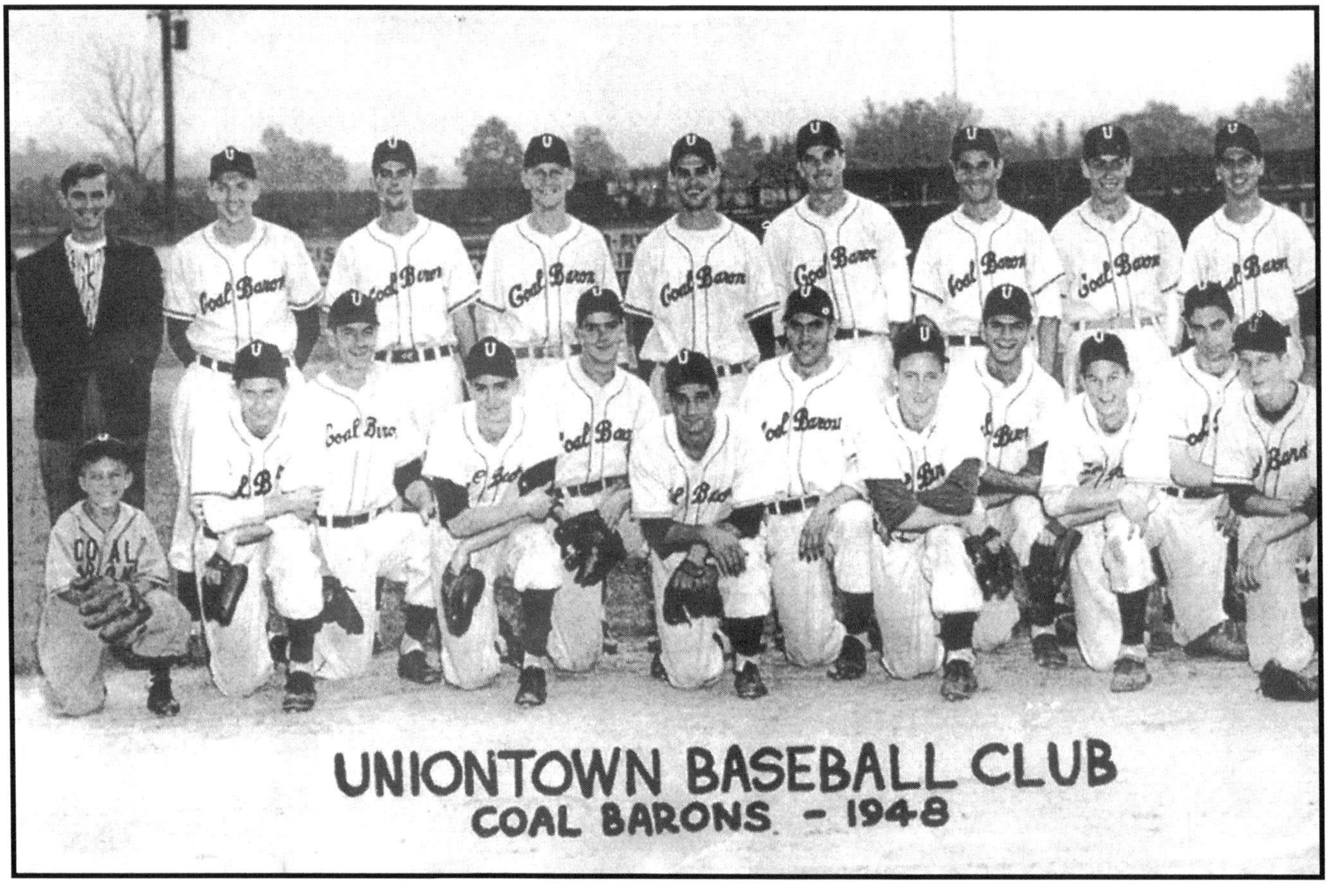
UNIONTOWN BASEBALL CLUB
COAL BARONS - 1948

Coal Baron team: Front row, center is Manager William Alfred Mongiello, 1948.

Calvin Grey Hogue was the pitcher for the Coal Barons. He autographed this photo to Dr. Regis M. Maher, M.D. of Uniontown.

L – R – Coal Baron President Harry Isabel, Manager Bill Mongiello. Business Manager, Chris Wagner, standing.

Newspapers rung with the following headline May 11, 1953:

## *Son of Local Race Track Owner Killed as 4,000 Look On*

Donald F. Guseman, 19, son of Uniontown Speedway owner William T. Guseman, met his death on the quarter mile dirt track May 10, 1953. The Gusemans built the track where today's Kennedy School resides and opened in the fall of 1952. With his family looking on, young Guseman took the lead by a quarter lap during the second lap of a twenty five lap feature event. He failed to negotiate a turn, rolled the car, and was thrown onto the track due to a faulty seat belt. Three stock cars swerved to miss him and the next two ran over the youth. He died of a fractured skull at 5:35pm in the Uniontown Hospital, shortly after he arrived there.

Guseman was one of thirteen drivers that fatal day. The others were: Don Kelly, Chris Shallenberger, "Bunk" Karzen, Cecil Hughes, Melvin Matlick, Bill Dull, Bill Kelly, John Zevo, Spike Woods, and Bob Burns.

Sam Shafer, brother-in-law of the victim was starter at the track. Due to a pile up at the beginning of the race, it was started over a second time with only 13 of the original 15 entries. Night racing was scheduled to start a few days after this race, but was cancelled. The upcoming Sunday race was run on time.

Donald's parents were William T. and Pearl Fitzsimmons Guseman. He was survived by three brothers, Earl R. of Uniontown; Airman Second Class Jesse J. who was in Alaska; and Private William T., Jr., who was stationed at Camp Carson, Colorado; and a Uniontown sister, Mrs. Stella Marie Shafer (wife of Starter).

Reverend Ronald Mosely, pastor at the Christ Methodist Church officiated burial at the Oak Lawn Cemetery after services at the Gleason Funeral Home.

Left is Mack Hinkle. William T. Guseman in suit. Car #101. Circa 1953.

Guseman's Uniontown Speedway with Walter Zitney on right.

Butts Butterball leans on his race car in the 1950's. Butts was a popular driver and sponsor around the Uniontown area. "Riding on Balls" was seen on many race cars for years in the area. He was also the owner of Speedway Auto Wreckers.

# *Mel Minnick, Sr. - Uniontown Driver Extraordinaire*

Four decades of racing began in 1949 for Mel Minnick, Sr. of Uniontown when he sat behind the wheel of a race car for the first time. "I was pretty lucky," Minnick says of his driving career which wowed race fans from the eastern United States for four decades. "I had good cars and sponsors who thought about the safety of the car," he said explaining how he survived so many close calls.

One of Mel's most memorable races was run in 1953 at Guseman's Uniontown Speedway. It was the work of the lucky number seven. He won seven separate races in seven different cars in one day. First he won a heat in his '33 Chevy Coup #13 Jr. The second heat was won in Jimmy Byers #319. The third was won in the Cornish Garage/Fish Carburator#M3. He then, after discussing with Bob Arsenberger the Ford V8 engine Minnick had sold him, took the checkered flag proving the motor was as good as he told Bob it was. He took the fifth race in #L1. The sixth heat was a six lap, six car helmet race which he won in car #98. The lucky seven race happened when Pop Cornish had Mel drive the 6 7/8 to a record win. Throughout the rest of that year, Minnick won three track championships.

That set Minnick up as the most aggressive driver in these parts, a reputation he went on to prove by winning over 500 feature races throughout his career. He competed in all local race tracks in addition to Indiana, in stock cars, coups, sprints, modifieds, supermodifieds, and late model cars. He even crossed the finish line upside down once at the Morgantown Speedway to win the feature in Bounce Hager's #35 Fun Seeker.

If that is not enough, to prove his tenacity, Minnick raced G.T. George's modified just days after being shot in the head in a fight for yet another victory. He was in intensive care when he went to the nurses station and demanded his I.V. be taken out because, "we are going racing tonight."

Minnick's sons, Mel Minnick, Jr. and Paul Craft, are now strong race car drivers at Motordrome. Mel, Sr., who has retired, is a great help in the pits and a treasure of knowledge and stories that can not be compared.

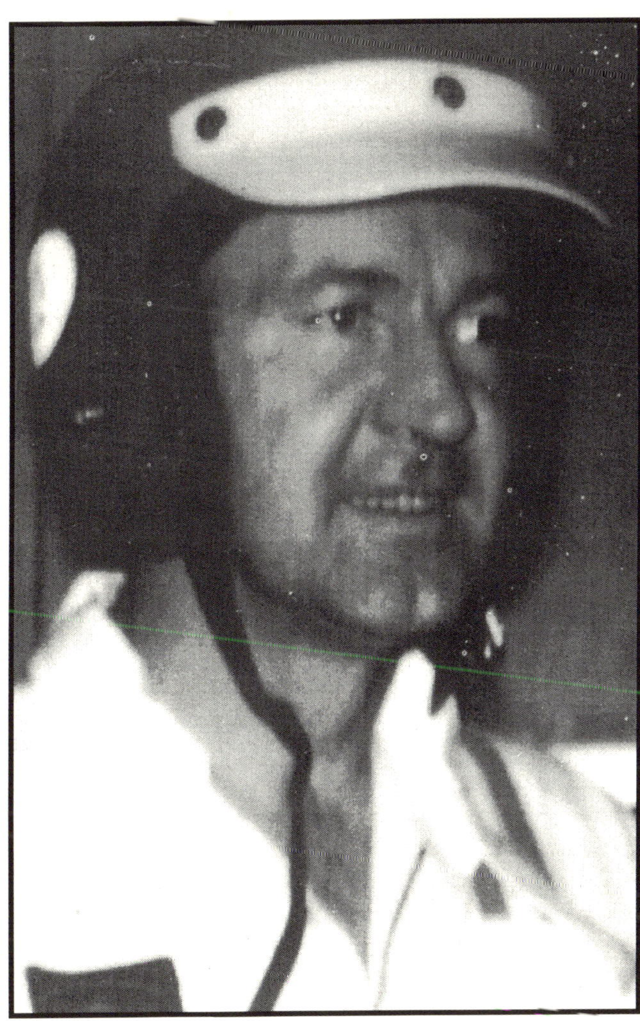

At age 47, Mel Minnick, Sr. had driven race cars for 27 years, thus far!

(top left photo ) Mel Minnick, Sr. winning another one early in his four decade career. Minnick drove this car for owners Bun and Jim Cornish of the Cornish Garage on Wine Street in Uniontown. 1955 photograph.
(second photo) Art "Pop" Cornish poses with the custom-built race car built by the Cornishes in the late 50's for Minnick to drive.
(third photo) Minnick and his buddy, the checkered flag. Circa 1964.
(fourth photo) While driving the Funseeker for Robert "Bounce" Hager, Minnick crossed the finish line in Morgantown a winner, upside down!
(fifth photo) Mel Minnick, Sr., 1958, at the Cornish Garage, 46 Wine Street, Uniontown. (Neener Masi's garage).

A super modified racer driven by Minnick for owner Mr. Lutz, 1964.
(second) Minnick goes for the money in a super modified "stretch midget" at the Latrobe Speedway in 1964.
(third) In 1996, Mel Minnick Sr. was inducted into the Pittsburgh Circle Track Club Hall of Fame. The ceremony was held January 27, 1996 at the Al Monza Palace in Monroeville, PA. Shown from left to right are: Minnick's son, Paul Craft, Mel Minnick, Sr., Don Gamble, Host of 1360-AM's Rappin' on Racin', and Mel Minnick, Jr., 1995 Pittsburgh Track Champion.

# About Author

Marci McGuinness is a southwestern Pennsylvania native. Her loves of Ohiopyle and the written word have led her to record local history, so that it is not lost in the "progress shuffle."

The author has written and published over 20 regional books and magazines since 1981. She also served as Marketing Director, then, Managing Editor, at the prestigious Cornell Maritime Press/Tidewater Publishers in Centreville, Maryland. There she published books by dozens of authors and professors on Chesapeake Bay and Maritime topics.

Today, McGuinness resides in Chalk Hill, Pennsylvania with her Jack Russell Terrier, Jake. She is presently launching reprints of all of her Yesteryear books in addition to the new title, *Yesteryear in Ohiopyle, Volume III.*

Under production for 2009 release are: *Gone to Ohiopyle, Haunted Laurel Highlands, Yesteryear in Ohiopyle, Volume IV and Murder in Ohiopyle and Other Tales.*

Visit her at ohiopyle.info or shorepublications.info.
Contact her at: shorepublications@yahoo.com.

# Books by Marci McGuinness

Gone to Ohiopyle (Coming Spring 2009)
How to be a Working Author/Writer (2005; 2nd Edition, Fall 2008)
Chesapeake Bay Blue Crabs (2004)
In it to Win It (2001)
The Explorer's Guide to the Youghiogheny River, Ohiopyle and SW PA Villages (2000)
Along the Baltimore & Ohio Railroad, from Cumberland to Uniontown (1998)
Stone House Legends & Lore (1998)
Yesteryear at the Uniontown Speedway (1996)
Official Program U.S.A. Speedway, 1916 Reprint (1996)
Yesteryear in Ohiopyle - The Movie
Yesteryear in Smithfield (1996)
Yesteryear in Masontown (1994)
Yesteryear in Ohiopyle and Surrounding Communities, Volume III (2008)
Yesteryear in Ohiopyle and Surrounding Communities, Volume II (1994)
Yesteryear in Ohiopyle and Surrounding Communities, Volume I (1993)
No Outlet! (1993)
Incidents (1992)
Nanny's Kitchen Cookbook (1991)
Natural Remedies, Recipes & Realities (1986)
The Deerhunter's Guide to Success...from the woods to the skillet (1985)
Natural Remedies (1984)
Unforgettable Poems for Everyday People (1984)
What's Happenin' Around Ohiopyle (1981)

## More Publications by McGuinness

Around Ohiopyle Magazine (Launched 2008)
Tying the Knot Magazine (2007)
St. Michaels/Tilghman Coupon Booklet (2003)
Yesteryear Calendar series (1990's)
Speak Easy Digest (1990's)
Naturally Yours Newsletter (1980's)

## Web Sites by Marci McGuinness

www.ohiopyle.info; www.shorepublications.info; www.marcimcguinness.com;
www.aroundohiopyle.com, www.positivelypublished.com, www.uniontownspeedway.com

Made in the USA
Charleston, SC
25 September 2011